Praise for *The Stra Workout*

'A practical and highly useful "how to" manual for developing the all-important strategy for any organisation. This is a must-read for anyone starting out in management, and would be useful even at senior management and board level.'

Geoff Peters, CEO, Moore DM Group and
Chairman, CDR Fundraising Group USA

'This is the book I wish I'd when a junior manager keen to make my way in complex organisations. It's clear and insightfully covers all the big issues and techniques.'

Peter Hewitt, Chief Executive, Guy's and St Thomas' Charity

'The first step in any strategy is to read this book! Ross and Segal present a concise, accessible and thorough read and offer all the tools you need to contribute to strategy.'

Tim Reed, CEO, Health Action International, Holland

'So many people are intimidated by strategy, and particularly by books about how to create it. This one takes the fear away and cuts through the waffle that often surrounds strategy development. It's particularly good for emerging managers who want to contribute more but aren't sure how. I'd also recommend to those who have done it so many times before it's gotten stale – this is a good refresher.'

Caroline Harper PhD, CEO, Sightsavers International

The Strategy Workout

The Strategy Workout

The 10 tried-and-tested steps that will build your strategic thinking skills

Bernard Ross and Clare Segal

PEARSON

Harlow, England • London • New York • Boston • San Francisco • Toronto • Sydney
Auckland • Singapore • Hong Kong • Tokyo • Seoul • Taipei • New Delhi
Cape Town • São Paulo • Mexico City • Madrid • Amsterdam • Munich • Paris • Milan

Pearson Education Limited
Edinburgh Gate
Harlow CM20 2JE
United Kingdom
Tel: +44 (0)1279 623623
Web: www.pearson.com/uk

First edition published 2016 (print and electronic)

ISBN: 978–1–292–08462–6 (print)
978–1–292–08464–0 (PDF)
978–1–292–08463–3 (eText)
978–1–292–08465–7 (ePub)·

British Library Cataloguing-in-Publication Data
A catalogue record for the print edition is available from the British Library

Library of Congress Cataloging-in-Publication Data
A catalog record for the print edition is available from the Library of Congress

10 9 8 7 6 5 4 3 2 1
19 18 17 16 15

Cover design by Two Associates
Print edition typeset in 10/13 Scene Std by 71
Print edition printed and bound in Great Britain by Henry Ling Ltd, at the Dorset Press, Dorchester, Dorset

NOTE THAT ANY PAGE CROSS REFERENCES REFER TO THE PRINT EDITION

Contents

About the authors   xii
Acknowledgements   xiii
Introduction   xiv
Self-assessment questionnaire   xxii

**PART 1   10 steps to becoming a more
           strategic thinker   1**

Step 1   Join the conversation:
         thinking and talking strategy   3

Learn how to join in strategic conversations with senior colleagues. Understand some of the key ideas needed to take part in strategic conversations. Discover if you are a Spock or Kirk, in strategic terms.

Step 2   Strategy stress test: getting
         the fundamentals right   17

Put in place the four key elements of a strategy: vision, mission, values and competencies. Explore how to stress test your company's vision and how to make sure your values are aligned and enforced. Discover the cost of getting it all wrong.

Step 3   Sort out stuff: clarifying the real situation   29

Clarify WBAWIN (what business are we in) and what are the rules of the business game you want to play.

Learn to use the analysis tools you acquire on day one at Harvard Business School.

Step 4   Do not sweat the small stuff:
dealing with what is important   40
Make sure you focus on what is important, using one of three frameworks: Delphic, MoSCoW and Fact + Implication Drivers. Summarise this focus by creating internal and external drivers from facts and implications.

Step 5   Imagine possibilities:
thinking like a futurologist   53
Put aside strategic hindsight and, instead, use strategic foresight. Use the six steps of scenario planning to identify possible futures and then work out what you might do to make them come true.

Step 6   Know your enemy: assessing
the competition   63
Establish who the competition is and how they compete. Work out what your value proposition is. Learn to use the Five Forces Model to work out whether to enter or exit from a market successfully.

Step 7   Focus your energy:
making the right choices   72
Essentially, you have only four strategic choices in terms of future direction. The challenge is deciding how to make the right one – balancing risk and payoff. We share 5Cs to help you make the choice.

Step 8   Think outside the box: using
innovation to develop new ideas   82
Marketing guru Philip Kotler says that innovation is the *only* sustainable competitive advantage. Discover how to develop innovative ideas using three flipcharts and six hats for different ways of thinking.

Step 9 Explore the territory:
building a strategy map   **95**

Understand how to build a strategy map and balanced scorecard that will give practical, easy-to-understand actions for you and the whole team. Use how/why logic to ensure that the logic is solid and joined up.

Step 10 Maintain momentum:
turning ideas into action   **106**

This step explores how to ensure that any strategy you develop actually happens. The core elements are 3Ms: momentum, motivation and metrics. For metrics, we show how to develop lead and lag indicators.

PART 2 10 strategy skills in action   **115**

Skill 1   Entering the dragon's den:
pitching your idea   **117**

Skill 2   Transmitting on WIFM:
the world's favourite radio station   **122**

Skill 3   Creating a burning platform:
explaining difficult choices   **126**

Skill 4   Absolutely fabulous: planning
strategy PR   **129**

Skill 5   Think, feel, do: getting your
message across   **134**

Skill 6   Creating your strategy A Team:
putting together talent   **137**

Contents

Skill 7   Meeting the black swan:
          thinking the unthinkable   140

Skill 8   Resistance is futile: overcoming the 5Cs   145

Skill 9   Strategic swimming: are you like
          a shark or a whale?   151

Skill 10   Strategy stylist: keeping up
          with fashionable gurus   156

PART 3 10 strategy challenges in action   161

Challenge 1 Post mortem: how to learn
             when a strategy goes wrong   163

Challenge 2 #me: how to develop
             powerful personal branding   168

Challenge 3 Think fast and slow:
             how to make difficult choices   174

Challenge 4 Pivot: how to change
             the plan on the move   178

Challenge 5 Look and learn: how to work
             with consultants   182

Challenge 6 Smarter strategy: how to
             develop double loop learning   185

Challenge 7 Careful! How to manage
             organisational risk   189

Challenge 8 Mind your back: how to
             manage personal risk   194

Challenge 9 Only 24 hours: how to balance
             short- and long-term priorities   197

Challenge 10 Napkin-based strategy: how
             to explain your idea informally   202

Build your development plan:
growing your strategic mindset and skillset   205

Self-assessment questionnaire   212
What have you learned?
What can you put into practice today?
How will you do it?

Index   216

About the authors

Bernard Ross is also a director of The Management Centre. He has worked with many of the world's largest International Non-Governmental Organisations (INGOs) and companies on strategic issues, from The International Federation of Red Cross and Red Crescent to The Tate Gallery and HSBC. Bernard is the author of three previous books – two of them co-authored with Clare. His most recent book, *Global Fundraising: How the World is Changing the Rules of Philanthropy*, won the Skystone Partners AFP Research Prize for Research.

Clare Segal is a director of The Management Centre, Europe's leading consultancy for ethical organisations. Clare's early career was as an award-winning video and film maker. She now oversees the learning and development programme at The Management Centre and offers coaching on communications to senior executives. Clare is the author of three previous books, one of which, *Breakthrough Thinking,* won the prestigious Terry McAdam Prize for best non-profit management book in the USA – the only time a European has won the prize.

Acknowledgements

Thanks to the great production team at Pearson Education for their help and encouragement: Nicole Eggleton, Eloise Cook and Melanie Carter. Thanks also to our colleagues at =mc for their ideas and inspiration.

Publisher's acknowledgements

We are grateful to the following for permission to use copyright material:

Photo on page 8 courtesy of CBS Photo archive/ Getty Images; photo on page 131 by Jakub Krechowicz.

'Amazon's leadership values' on pages 25–6 reprinted courtesy of Amazon.com, Inc. and its affiliates.

In some cases we have been unable to trace the owners of copyright material, and we would appreciate any information that would enable us to do so.

Introduction

Welcome to *The Strategy Workout*

Thank you for investing in this book and, by doing that, investing in yourself. We hope you will find that your investment delivers exactly what it says on the cover.

- **Strategy:** a plan of action designed to deliver a long-term significant impact or result.
- **Workout:** a place to improve overall fitness through a series of exercises and activities.

So, we have written this book for anyone who is ambitious to succeed in becoming more strategic in the way they think and act and who is prepared to work hard to develop the skills and knowledge they need for that success. If that's you then we are delighted to have the chance to work with you.

We guess you might be wondering why you need to be a better strategist to succeed. Is being smart and willing not enough? Well, anyone who compared the strategy choices of the major political parties at the 2015 UK General Election might agree that bad strategic choices, all made by smart and willing people, can lead to loss of power. Good analysis and strategic choices can mean a transformation in your ability to succeed.

There are other concrete reasons to invest in your strategic ability. As someone able to think and act strategically you will:

- identify the key issues your team or organisation needs to address
- be welcomed into project teams as someone who adds value
- handle changes of plan, even radical ones, smoothly

- offer senior managers insights, no matter where you are in the hierarchy
- come up with imaginative solutions to difficult problems
- be able to explain complex problems – mostly on the back of a napkin

and maybe even:

- secure the chance to head up initiatives and, perhaps, secure promotion.

The workout of the title is a workout for your mind. So we have packed these pages full of frameworks and ideas to help you improve the way you look at problems and how you shape and share solutions. The good news is you can start more or less anywhere and enjoy the strategic workout in that section. If you are looking for inspiration, try **Step 5** on futurology. If you are ready for weird stuff, try **Skill 7** on black swans. If you need to try something different in a rush, plunge into **Challenge 4** on pivoting. And if you do not mind some hard work in the gym, then **Steps 1–4** will give you the fundamentals.

The book is designed to be interactive, so we have included a number of self-help assessments and exercises to ensure you gain maximum benefit. You can work through these at your own pace and in your own time. Watch out for online resources, too.

As you work through the activities and exercises, we guarantee they will help you become a more able, faster, clearer strategist – no matter where you currently are in the hierarchy of your company, your department or your team. We have put together the exercises and activities based on our experience of working with large organisations in the private, public and voluntary sectors of the economy – from John Lewis Partnership to the International Red Cross and Red Crescent and from the OECD to the BBC. These approaches worked for them and they will work for you.

We have organised the book, like others in the series, into Steps, Actions and Challenges. Each of these elements offers a different kind of insight and, together, they will help you develop the skillset and mindset to ensure that you can hold your own on any strategic discussion or add value in any strategic project. It might even help you to come up with some radical and profitable entrepreneurial ideas of your own.

- The **10 steps** cover the building blocks you need for a strategy – the key frameworks and tools you need to shape strategic thinking. You do not need to read them in sequence, but we recommend you try **Steps 1** and **2** to gain early understanding.
- The **10 actions** are a chance to apply some strategic ideas to particular situations you might face. And we look especially at how to build your credibility and communicate strategic ideas quickly and powerfully.
- The **10 challenges** will help you face up to particularly difficult situations – when things seem to be going wrong or you are worried they might go wrong. Head there if you need practical advice on how to overcome a challenge.

A route map into the book – the 6Cs of strategy

The book is organised so you can read it in chunks. The good news is you do not have to read it in strict sequence. But, before you plunge into the contents too deeply, if you asked us to summarise the book, we would say that the book, and strategy itself, was about six overarching Cs:

1. Customers
2. Context
3. Competencies
4. Competition
5. Commitment
6. Companions.

Let us relate those 6Cs to the different sections of the book, offering a route in.

Working out who your customers are

Successful business strategy always begins and ends with making sure you meet the interests and needs of customers and consumers. (Customers = people who buy your offerings; consumers = people who use them.) Everything that does not begin and end in this is no more than an interesting academic discussion. It is customers and their cumulative purchases that make for business results – especially profit.

To succeed in meeting those needs, you need to be clear about whose interests you seek to serve and how you serve them. In **Step 7** Focus your energy, we talk about the four key options you have in terms of matching up these customers and offerings.

If you are keen to think more about this topic of customers and their needs, make sure you read **Step 6** on competitors and, if you want to know more, read **Challenge 4** on pivoting.

Getting to grips with the context

Of course, the context you operate in can significantly impact on your value proposition or your ability to deliver it.

So, context covers a number of issues, from the possible opportunities and risks in your business model to the legislative and social setting in which you have to work, to the market conditions you might experience – and many more in between. If you are keen to explore context more fully, head straight for **Steps 3, 4** and **6.**

Sometimes, the context is frighteningly simple – and scary. When that happens, you may need to talk about a burning platform – a situation that needs urgent and dramatic action for any chance of a positive outcome. To find out more about how to handle these – and even how to use them to your advantage – look at **Skill 3** on burning platforms.

If you are keen on how to make action stick, look at **Step 10** on momentum. And if you want to learn from previous actions, consider adopting the approach in **Challenge 6** on double loop learning.

Making sure you have the right competencies

Another major issue in strategy today is competencies – what skills, knowledge and abilities does your company, department, or even your team, have? And, as important, which ones does it need to develop? This is especially important in a volatile world where the ability to change and adapt is central to success.

As you gaze into the future, you may imagine a possible need for some quite radical new competencies or approaches. To consider how you might need to change or adapt, review the ideas and models in **Step 5** on futurology, **Step 8** on thinking outside the box and **Skill 7**, where you will learn how to deal with the truly unexpected – black swans as they are known.

Even in an established or relatively stable context, there are detailed questions to answer about competencies. What experience do you have, or need, to launch a new offering? Do you know the best channel mix to use for the new strategy? Launching into an initiative without the necessary competencies will end in tears, unless you can learn fast on the job.

Finally, note that competencies do not exist in a vacuum. They form part of a key framework – vision, mission, values and competencies – which is explored fully in **Step 2**. While competencies may change, in general vision, mission and values do not – and should not – change. You may want to assess your vision, mission and values here, too.

Dealing with the competition

If only you could devise and implement a strategy by yourself without concern for others. Sadly, this is not the case. A pivotal question in any strategy is to consider who else is in the space you would like to occupy or explore – and how strong are they? Linked to this, how can you gain or maintain a competitive edge?

We can redefine the nature of competition by considering two kinds of strategic competition – red ocean and blue ocean. In a red ocean, you need to compete head to head with a rival that has their eyes on the same market. But, in blue ocean, you try to redefine the rules, and even the game you play, to put as much competitive distance as possible between you and any rivals. Find out more about this distinction by reading **Skill 9**, which looks in more detail at these two options.

And, if you need a rigorous framework to tackle red ocean competition, then do not miss out on Michael Porter's Five Forces in **Step 6** about competition.

Securing emotional and rational commitment

Commitment is about gaining the emotional and, perhaps, financial engagement of some key stakeholders, including you.

To succeed in gaining commitment, you need to address the right issues with the right people. Have a look at **Step 3** Sort out stuff. If you have identified these issues correctly, almost certainly you will know who they will affect and, therefore, who you need to target.

A second strand to gaining commitment may require you to change yourself and act more like a strategic player. This means changing your own attitude, behaviour or communication approach and thinking about you as a brand. See **Challenge 2** for turning yourself into a brand and **Skill 5** Think, feel, do.

You need to consider how you will respond to challenges to your proposal. Have a look at the key tactics in **Skill 8** on overcoming resistance to your idea.

Getting the right companions

The final C concerns your companions – or what would, more often, be called stakeholders.

At its heart, strategy is just a set of ideas until people put it into action. Throughout the book, we look at the importance of bringing different stakeholders on board – and keeping them on board. These people can include: the board, senior managers, peers, team members and even colleagues in other departments. To engage and align all your stakeholders, you will need good communication skills. We look at a whole range of these in **Step 9** Explore the territory and in **Skill 1** Entering the dragon's den: pitching your idea.

You also need to surround yourself with the right people – engaging and aligning various talents and abilities to complement your own. For some hints on how to do that, pay attention to **Skill 6** Creating your strategy A Team.

You will, almost certainly, meet and work with consultants at some point – make sure you use them well. See **Challenge 5** Look and learn: how to work with consultants.

We have laid out the book in a broad sequence, so you can use it in different ways:

- Read it all the way through – there are common threads to spot.
- Dip in to solve a specific challenge or skill to address a concrete issue.
- Share with a coach as you work on various practical issues.

As you read it, you will see some symbols to help direct your attention:

Activity   **Key idea**   **Media**

Assess yourself: building the strategic mindset and skillset

Take out your mobile phone. Have a look at it. In your hands you have an almost definitive insight to the world of changing strategy.

Ten years ago, your phone would have been made by one of the giants – Ericsson, Nokia or BlackBerry. Now those names have all but disappeared – overtaken by Samsung and Apple, which decided it would be a good idea to get into mobile telephony. The old companies were not unproductive – they were working hard and making big decisions about hardware, software and design. They just made the wrong decisions. . . while the newbies made some very good decisions, even with no experience of the market or the technology.

Some companies make good strategic decisions and some make poor ones. Or, more accurately, some *people* in companies make good strategic decisions and some make very poor ones. This book is designed to help you contribute to the good decisions at whatever level you can – personally, in your team, in your department or even across the whole company.

To succeed, you need more than just the ability to do what you already do better. You need not just a strategic skillset – the knowledge of *how* to do something – but also a mindset that questions *why* and *what*. This book is designed to help you develop that mindset and that skillset.

Self-assessment questionnaire

Before you dive into the book, take a moment to reflect. This questionnaire will guide you on your overall strategic ability – and guide you to where to focus your attention to achieve improvements.

1. **How confident are you to express your ideas in a strategic discussion?**

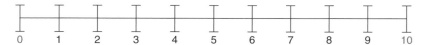

   Want to improve your score? Look at **Step 1 + Challenges 2, 10**

2. **How easily can you use strategic tools to analyse your current situation?**

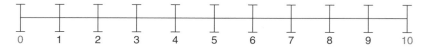

   Want to improve your score? Look at **Steps 2, 3 + Skills 9, 10**

3. **How easy do you find it to imagine alternative big picture futures?**

   Want to improve your score? Look at **Steps 5, 8 + Skill 7 + Challenge 4**

4. **How sure are you that you can identify who is key in your strategy?**

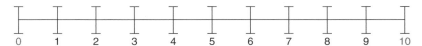

Want to improve your score? Look at **Step 6 + Skills 2, 6** and **8**

5. **How clear are you on how to turn strategy into step-by-step action?**

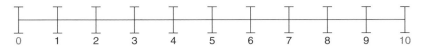

Want to improve your score? Look at **Steps 7, 9 + Skills 9, 10**

6. **How happy are you selling challenging ideas to others?**

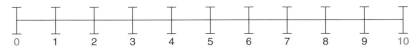

Want to improve your score? Look at **Steps 4, 10 + Skills 1, 2, 3 + Challenges 2, 6**

7. **How able are you to identify where to focus your energy and intellect?**

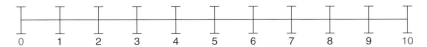

Want to improve your score? Look at **Step 7 + Skill 3 + Challenges 6, 9**

8. **How able are you to think the unthinkable and respond to it?**

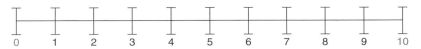

Want to improve your score? Look at **Steps 2, 3 + Skills 9, 10**

9. How ready are you to identify and deal with sources of resistance?

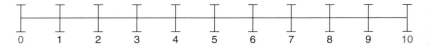

Want to improve your score? Look at **Steps 2, 3 + Skills 9, 10**

10. How confident are you to name and explain the work of strategic gurus?

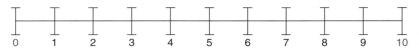

Want to improve your score? Look at **Step 1 + Skills 9, 10 + Challenge 5**

11. How strong and positive is your personal brand?

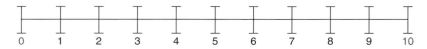

Want to improve your score? Look at **Step 9 + Skill 4 + Challenges 7, 8**

12. How sure are you that you can manage risk – personal and organisational?

Want to improve your score? Look at **Step 3 + Skill 3 + Challenges 7, 8**

13. Can you use strategic tools confidently to analyse your current situation?

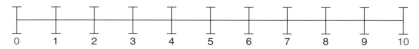

Want to improve your score? Look at **Steps 2, 3, 7 + Skills 9, 10 + Challenge 5**

14. How sure are you that you can manage organisational risk?

Want to improve your score? Look at **Steps 2, 3 + Skill 7 + Challenges 9, 10**

15. How good are you at expressing complex ideas simply and clearly?

Want to improve your score? Look at **Steps 1, 9 + Skills 1, 5 + Challenge 7**

Part 1

10 steps to becoming a more strategic thinker

Step 1   Join the conversation: thinking and talking strategy

Step 2   Strategy stress test: getting the fundamentals right

Step 3   Sort out stuff: clarifying the real situation

Step 4   Do not sweat the small stuff: dealing with what is important

Step 5   Imagine possibilities: thinking like a futurologist

Step 6   Know your enemy: assessing the competition

Step 7   Focus your energy: making the right choices

Step 8   Think outside the box: using innovation to develop new ideas

Step 9   Explore the territory: building a strategy map

Step 10 Maintain momentum: turning ideas into action

Step 1

Join the conversation: thinking and talking strategy

After reading this step you will be able to:

- Be clear on what it means to think and talk strategically
- Hold your own in a meeting where senior people are discussing strategy
- Explain to anyone else what the different elements in strategy are
- Understand the difference between key strategic terms.

Speak up, speak out

It is day one in your new job. You are in a team meeting. It all seems to be going well and then the senior manager in the room announces, 'Let's get out of the weeds here and start sorting out a new business approach. I'm looking for fresh strategic thinking . . .' So, one voice in your left ear says, 'This is your big chance, take it.' And another voice in your right ear says, 'Be careful, this could go seriously wrong.' What do you do?

Part of the secret of success in this situation is to join the conversation and show that, no matter how new you are to the business, you can think strategically and contribute to a strategic conversation. This step will help you hold your own and, maybe, even impress.

If you are looking for inspiration, you might like to check out this list of 25 entrepreneurs under the age of 30 who have set up companies worth over $100 m at the time of writing: www.businessinsider.com/young-successful-entrepreneur-world-digital-100-2011-9. There are some well-known names, like Facebook's Zuckerberg, but you would be surprised how many you do not know. All of these people, at some point, spoke up – some of them even changed the conversation.

How do I know if I am thinking strategically?

We are sure you have met and been impressed by people who spoke confidently and fluently on a topic. If you want to impress others and win them over to your ideas, you need to learn to speak the language of strategy with the same confidence and fluency. (And, if you go to the gym, you need to get to know the difference between aerobic and anaerobic exercise, between cardio and stamina training.)

A key challenge you face, however, in deciding whether you are thinking and talking strategically, is that there is not a clear set of shared terms. There is not even a common agreed definition of the simple word strategy. Go to a bookshop and there are hundreds of volumes on the topic. Worse still, many of these books claim to hold the one truth in terms of a specific approach. But, to be honest, they cannot all be right and, anyway, we are keen to avoid dogma and prescription here.

'The first task of any theory is to clarify the terms and concepts that are confused... only after the terms and concepts have been agreed can we hope to consider the issues easily and clearly...'

Clausewitz, *On War*, 1833

'The first step in developing strategy is to lock the managers in a room and have them debate what is meant by a vision statement and how exactly it differs from a mission statement. This is important because one wrong move and employees will start doing "vision" things when they should be doing "mission" things and before long it will be impossible to sort it all out...'

Scott Adams, *The Dilbert Principle*, 1996

We are practical consultants working on strategic issues with large and small clients every day. Our mission is to equip you with a host of tools and frameworks that you will need to hold your own in a strategic discussion and that will enable you to form and share your views and approaches.

Despite the caveat above on no one definition, we are going to start by offering you our simple pragmatic definition:

 Strategy is 'a set of decisions designed to develop and deliver a specific long-term, significant outcome'.

This means you can have strategy at lots of different levels but always answering a question:

- **An entire organisation:** 'In what direction should we take this company to ensure success?'
- **A specific product, service or offering:** 'How should we adapt this offering to help it achieve its potential impact?'
- **A department or function:** 'What kind of HR strategy should we have to ensure that we attract and hold on to high-performing people?'
- **You can even have a personal one:** 'How should I systematically build my career to ensure I make the most of opportunities?'

5

So you can be strategic at many levels. And, as we try to illustrate throughout the book, you can be strategic running a corner café or a multi-million-pound engineering company, a local authority or a humanitarian NGO.

Are you thinking like a strategist? A checklist

Let us make this simpler still. You are probably thinking strategically if you do four things:

1. You make your decisions after assessing information and weighing up different possibilities for action.
2. The decisions commit you as an individual, a group or organisation to specific steps.
3. These steps follow some kind of logic or sequence and are designed to deliver a specific trackable outcome.
4. The outcome has a significant impact and represents a longer-term commitment.

So, if you are having a conversation with these characteristics or thinking thoughts with these characteristics . . . congratulations! You are being strategic.

Global and local

Strategy can be as high level as Apple deciding to take a decade to build its presence in the music and entertainment field by making a series of significant, billion-dollar investments in hardware and software innovations.

Or it can be as basic as a café owner choosing to offer coffee and pastry deals in the morning to regular customers to improve their customer base long term and to increase their average spend.

In both cases, notice the four principles above in action – 'Based on what we know, if we do this, and this, and this, then that will deliver that significant result.' And, in general, strategy involves more than one person taking action – Apple needs a Steve Jobs for marketing genius *and* a Jony Ives for design genius. (It also needs a Tim Cook to build on the strategy after Jobs is gone.) And the humblest café owner needs their staff to understand their role in supporting their strategy of upselling beyond the basic cup of coffee to commuters – and to tell them what they know of commuters suggesting that bacon butties would sell better than pastries.

Choose your conversation companions – stakeholders

To make it happen, strategy generally needs a range of people on board – at the very least understanding what you are trying to do. Generally, we call these individuals and groupings stakeholders. For the moment, let us define a stakeholder as an individual or group who has a legitimate interest in the affairs of an organisation. So, stakeholders could include external ones like customers, consumers, regulators, the Government, suppliers, trade unions and the media; or internal ones like team members, fellow employees, managers, the board and shareholders, etc.

At a team level, they could include your manager, colleagues and other teams you serve as internal customers. If you want to explore this idea more, make sure you look at **Step 4** and **Challenge 2** of the book where we explore the idea of stakeholder mapping in more detail. For the moment, think about who you should be listening and talking to.

Are you Spock or Kirk? Choosing your strategy preference

We are sure you are familiar with one or more of the incarnations of the *Star Trek* film franchise. Two of the characters stand out for their approach to some of the big issues they need to tackle. And they have very different approaches to strategy.

- **Kirk** is famous for leaps of intuition and ambitious have-a-go action.
- **Spock** tends to represent the logical approach through rational analysis.

Source: CBS Photo Archive/Getty Images

It might appear that we are suggesting all strategy is a simple, logical progression – a Spock-type journey from B to A. But, let us be clear there may be times when you want to try a more Kirk-ish intuitive approach. (Think of how often Kirk's illogical moves outwit the enemy.) Do not be afraid to explore both approaches when developing strategy. And, remember, the main learning from the films, and even the cult original TV show, is that they are a great team because they combine both approaches. When you are considering contributing a strategic idea, do not be afraid to share logic and intuition. But also notice when you are in a group what the preference of the others in the room are and be aware of how your preference might impact.

If you are a fan of the intuitive approach, you will also find some support for this from one of our favourite management gurus, Henry Mintzberg. One of his big ideas is to make a distinction between *planning* and *crafting* strategy. The metaphor he uses is that of a potter. A potter, he says, gets their hands dirty and improvises based on the here and now, building on mental and physical engagement with the work they are doing. In the same way, he says, it is impossible to separate the formulation and implementation of strategy – for him it is a continuous and adaptive process. When planned strategy meets the real world, he talks about emergent strategy. Scenario planning, covered in **Step 5**, fits absolutely into the crafting model. **Step 9**, covering the Kaplan and Norton strategy map, is much more planning-based.

Take a minute to think about the two approaches and maybe establish your own preference. Are you a Spock or a Kirk by preference?

Planning strategy: the Spock approach	Crafting strategy: the Kirk approach
You are more like a Spock strategist if you like: • a formalised system using a specific sequence of models and frameworks • calendar-based planning • thinking led by a senior leader • analysis and hard data • extrapolating from the past • intellectually thinking things through • left-brain, logical risk analysis • sticking to the plan.	**You are more like a Kirk strategist if you like:** • an informal approach with various models and frameworks • reviewing the process as necessary • everyone engaged in a process • synthesising ideas and feelings • searching for future discontinuities • pragmatic responsive doing • right-brain, creative, intuitive effort • adopting opportunistic changes.

OK, now you know which you are, make sure you are aware of the preferences of the others you are trying to influence. You may need to adapt your preference!

Mind your language

So, now you know your preference. But you need to share a clear basic common language to frame the conversation with your colleagues – especially senior ones. (And, no matter how senior you are, you are unlikely to deliver a strategy by yourself.)

It helps if you understand how the different bits of a strategy fit together. Have a look at the diagram below. It explains some of the key ideas common in strategy using the metaphor of a road along which a team or organisation travels towards its strategic destination.

The key elements in our map metaphor are a vision, mission, values and competencies. Together they form a (VMVC) framework. Every organisation, department and team should have one of these. You might even consider having one for yourself. (There is more about this framework in **Step 2**.)

Together they represent the key elements that allow you to organise your or others' key ideas in a systematic and strategic way.

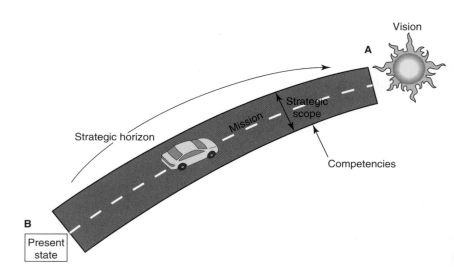

Let us look at each of these elements and see how they fit together. As we go through it, consider whether your organisation or team has each element in place.

 To see an animation of how the various elements in strategy build up see our video here:

www.thebusinessgym.net

Where you want to get to, aka vision (A)

At one end of the diagram is a *vision* – a positive future your organisation, department or team is working to create. Strategies are simply a way to deliver visions. This is the destination for your strategy. It should not focus on what you do, it should focus on the result or outcome you want. A great vision serves to mobilise individual and team efforts in a unified direction. All of your stakeholders have to get the vision.

A good vision is probably the single most important element in a strategy. In **Step 2** we will show you what a good vision statement looks like and help you to write one.

Where you want to get to, aka present state (B)

At the other end of the road is the present state (or current situation). Almost all strategy involves analysis of where you are now and how good or bad that situation is. There are several well-known, useful tools typically used to deliver this analysis, such as PEST, SWOT or benchmarking.

For more information on these various tools see **Steps 2** and **3**. Included in the present state analysis is a bit of history and previous results. Often the past is a good guide to the future. But pay attention to **Step 5** on futurology where you will discover that the past does not always predict the future.

How to make the journey, aka strategy

Think of the road itself as the strategy. It describes your journey from B (the present state, where you are now) to A (your vision or where you want to be). All the other terms and phrases used in strategy discussions represent elements of the journey along this road. We have outlined a few of these key ideas below. And more are explained throughout the book.

How long do you need for thinking things over, aka strategic horizon?

At the top of the diagram there is a curved arrow indicating the strategic horizon: the period over which your strategy should

11

be considered. The length of the horizon varies from industry to industry. A pharmaceutical company can take 15 years to develop a new drug for cancer. This means that, to have a successful strategy, it needs to be capable of thinking through that span of time. On the other hand, the ups and downs and rapid changes of the music business mean that, if you are impresario Simon Cowell, your strategic horizon might be as little as six months.

Think about the business you are in: what is the strategic horizon? Do you and your colleagues really think over this period? Is there a conflict with other stakeholders' horizons? (We are sure you have heard many business people complaining about short-termism among shareholders.)

What is your basic approach, aka mission?

A mission is a statement of how an organisation will achieve its vision or its overarching business purpose. While the vision sets out the destination, the mission explains the general method or route.

So, missions tend to be much more about how to *do* strategy. Some are grand and global and designed to be inspiring. See the case study below for the headline mission of one of our favourite consultancy customers, Doctors Without Borders (Médecins Sans Frontières, MSF).

Some missions – despite the agency being at a global scale – are very practical. The finance department of Hillshire Brands, formerly Sara Lee, the global food manufacturer, has the following mission:

> *'To continuously add value to the company and colleagues by providing objective and innovative audit services that evaluate risk, control and governance processes.'*

In this case, the finance team's mission fits within the more general mission of the overall company, which is:

> *'To simply delight you . . . every day.'*

Notice how practical and clear these statements are.

Does anyone care?

Some companies devote time and resources to communicating strategy to employees. But, according to research at the University of Technology in Sydney, only a minority of employees take all this stuff in. Researchers asked employees of 20 major Australian corporations with clearly articulated public strategies to identify their employer's strategy from amongst six choices. Only 29 per cent answered correctly. (The good news is: the firms in the sample are all high performers, suggesting that a company can thrive, even if employees are clueless about its long-term vision.)

Harvard Business Review, June 2013

What are your core beliefs, aka values?

The strategy road is bounded by values and competencies. Values are beliefs, principles and attitudes that underpin an organisation's work.

The role of values in strategy is to help inform decisions about what you should or should not do. Organisations develop values about:

- the kind of culture they aspire to have
- the amount of risk they accept
- how they raise and spend money
- how they want their people to work
- the kind of customers they seek to serve
- the methodology they favour
- the way they work with suppliers.

So, interestingly, in the following MSF case study, it is clear they work with everyone in need – even the bad guys in a conflict. And, in the Sara Lee example, objective audits suggest that they will deliver uncomfortable truths, if necessary.

13

What do you need to be good at, aka competencies?

Competencies – the other boundary on the road – are defined as the skills, knowledge or abilities we have or need to achieve the strategy. There will be some activities an organisation is able to deliver, some it will have to gain the ability to deliver, and some it will be unable to deliver.

Setting out the core organisational competencies defines the abilities required to successfully deliver the strategy.

So, MSF has to have a core competence in different forms of emergency medicine – ranging from dealing with the injuries inflicted by wars to the care of people suffering from Ebola. They also need a core competence in logistics to get people and equipment into challenging locations fast – say after an earthquake.

Case study

Médecins Sans Frontières' strategy

MSF is one of the favourite customers we advise. It delivers extraordinary work at a global level. And, at the time of writing (May 2015), we are working on its global fundraising strategy. Here is its overall mission:

> MSF responds to emergencies and disasters and helps those in greatest need, providing medical aid to those most in need regardless of their race, religion, or political affiliation.

Notice the focus here is on medical support for emergencies and disasters. So, it does not deliver food aid, build emergency roads or even help develop sustainable long-term health systems. These are all useful things to do, but they are not part of MSF's mission so it does not do them.

See above for examples of MSF's values and competencies.

Case study

John Lewis' strategy

John Lewis is another one of our favourite consultancy customers. (And one of the UK's favourite suppliers.) It goes even further than almost any other company to detail how it does business with a written constitution that sets out its principles, governance system and rules. It does this for two reasons, as explained on its website:

> 'The first is historical. The John Lewis Partnership exists today because of the extraordinary vision and ideals of the Founder, John Spedan Lewis, who signed away his personal ownership rights in a growing retail company to allow future generations of employees to take forward his "experiment in industrial democracy". Not unreasonably, he wanted to leave some clear guidelines for his successors, so that the values which had motivated him would not be eroded with the passage of time.
>
> The second reason looks forward. Spedan Lewis was committed to establishing a "better form of business", and the challenge for Partners of today is to prove that a business which is not driven by the demands of outside shareholders and which sets high standards of behaviour can flourish in the competitive conditions of the third millennium.'

The John Lewis constitution actually states that 'the happiness of its members' is the Partnership's ultimate purpose. It establishes a system of 'rights and responsibilities', which places on all Partners the obligation to work for the improvement of the business in the knowledge that they share the rewards of success.

What can you do and not do, aka strategic scope?

Strategic scope is the range of acceptable activities between values and competencies – the width of the road. This represents the developmental space for an organisation or team – the range of things it will or might do.

Amazon is a good example of an organisation that began with quite a narrow strategic scope – simply selling books online. But, by developing its competencies – in IT, data analysis, distribution, marketing and partnering – it has been able to expand into a range of wider business areas. See **Step 2** for more on how Amazon has leveraged competencies to grow.

Call to action

- Are you ready and willing to speak up and speak out about strategic issues, even if you are not certain about the answer?
- Can you adapt your own preference for strategic ideas – Spock or Kirk – to match the preferences of the team you are working with?
- Are you clear what the key ideas and terms in strategy mean and can you come up with good examples of them?
- Can you see the various core strategic elements in place in your company or department?
- Are they memorable and do you see people really living and working by them? Do they guide daily action?

Step 2

Strategy stress test: getting the fundamentals right

After reading this step you will be able to:

- Know how to stress test a vision, mission, values and competencies (VMVC) framework
- Realise why these four elements are so important in strategy
- Understand how these elements are linked and impact on each other
- Construct a VMVC statement for your own team or department.

Is strategy really necessary?

To read any book on strategy, including this one, you would think that nothing could ever be achieved without a detailed written strategic framework. So you wonder how on earth Alexander the Great, born in 356 BC, managed to build an empire without a detailed strategy . . . far less a map. Remember that he was only 23 when he controlled most of the world – from Iraq to India and from Greece to Georgia. How on earth did he do that?

So, do you really need a strategy with lots of complicated models and frameworks? Will your organisation or team survive and thrive without it?

The answer is you probably need at least the most fundamental strategic framework – what we call a VMVC. A VMVC is the executive summary of any strategy – everything else is detail. With just these four elements you can achieve great things. Without them you might take lots of action, but it might be unfocused.

Returning to our gym metaphor, you need to have a framework for your fitness programme – do you want to look great on the beach, be able to run the London Marathon or just feel fitter?

You need to be clear on what you will or will not do to get that great body.

 Being clear on where you want to get to informs everything else.

Building a VMVC framework

As we saw in **Step 1**, the fundamental elements in a strategy are vision, mission, values and competencies. Every organisation should have these. But, even if you think you are unlikely to be writing a strategy for the whole business just yet, it is useful practice to write one for your team or department. (Or, if they already have one, it is useful to check it for consistency.)

Create an engaging vision

We discovered in **Step 1** that a vision is a statement of the positive, ultimate outcome or destination for your team, department or organisation. Vision statements can be long or short, detailed or general. There is no one right way to do one, though everyone has a theory. But a good vision will inform everything you and your colleagues do. If you do not have one, it might suggest that it does not matter *what* you do.

> *'Would you tell me, please, which way I ought to go from here?'*
>
> *'That depends a good deal on where you want to get to,' said the Cat.*
>
> *'I don't much care where,' said Alice.*
>
> *'Then it doesn't matter which way you go,' said the Cat.*
>
> *'–so long as I get SOMEWHERE,' Alice added as an explanation.*
>
> *'Oh, you're sure to do that,' said the Cat, 'if you only walk long enough.'*
>
> Lewis Carol, *Alice in Wonderland*, Chapter 6

How to stress test your company's vision statement

Let us assume that your company has a vision statement somewhere on the website, in the office manual or maybe on an aluminium plaque in reception. It should pass three tests if it is really to succeed in engaging stakeholders – including you.

Test 1: Is it engaging?

When you come in in the morning, does it make you think, 'Yep, that feels like something I really want to help do today'? See the wonderful Ford Motor Company case study below, which probably did have that effect. At the same time, avoid hype. For example, it always seems slightly odd to us that one famous UK company wants to be 'passionate about sandwiches'. (It is a piece of bread with a filling – get a life!)

Just as important, does the vision make customers think: 'Hmmm, they sound like the kind of people I'd like to do business with'?

Test 2: Is it simple?

Is it easy to explain to your grandmother or someone you meet in a bar? A vision should not be difficult to understand and should not use complex language. The best vision statements are demotic in style – that is, they can be spoken easily.

If it is a string of management buzzwords, clichés and insider language, then your company vision will fail this test. It seems, sometimes, that everything these days has to be 'world class', 'market-leading' and 'best-in-class'. This can be just junk language.

As is often the case, less is more. Microsoft had this vision: '. . . a computer on every desk'. (They managed to do pretty well.) Bob Geldof and his campaign with a three-word vision, 'Make Poverty History', engaged millions worldwide. Both these visions are really profound ideas expressed simply and memorably. That is your goal.

Test 3: Does it drive broad action?

A good vision should be meaningful to employees, obviously. But it should help partners, like suppliers and subcontractors, to deliver your vision. (See the PepsiCo vision statement below.) Internally, senior managers, managers, employees and even the board should recognise that it is their responsibility to help deliver on that vision.

Here is a vision statement that we think does not really drive appropriate action. Can you guess who they are?

> 'xxx is committed to building a family of the world's best fashion brands offering captivating customer experiences that drive long-term loyalty and deliver sustained growth for our shareholders.'*

*The answer is Victoria's Secret – how well does that describe working on what aims to be the world's sexiest lingerie brand?

Case study

Ford Motor Company: the vision thing

Vision statements can be long or short. The key criterion is how memorable and impactful it is. Even if not everyone can recite the statement word for word, it is important everyone knows the *essence* of it and believes it addresses them individually so they feel they are working to reach the same destination.

Henry Ford's vision of 1907 is a good example of a compelling vision:

> *'My vision is to build a motor car for the great multitude. It will be at so low a price that no man making a good salary will be unable to own one – and enjoy with his family the blessing of hours of pleasure in God's great open country. Everyone will have one. The horse will have disappeared from our highways and the automobile will be taken for granted.'*

Some visions might raise a wry smile when considering what the company actually does:

> *'PepsiCo's responsibility is to continually improve all aspects of the world in which we operate – environment, social, economic – creating a better tomorrow than today. Our vision is put into action through programs and a focus on environmental stewardship, activities to benefit society, and a commitment to build shareholder value by making PepsiCo a truly sustainable company.'*

Mission

A mission is a statement of how an organisation will achieve its vision or its overarching business purpose. While the vision sets out the destination, the mission explains the general method or route.

How to write a good mission statement

Good mission statements do not need to be fancy or poetic. At their simplest, they should include:

- **a strong action verb** – to enable, to deliver, to create, etc. – describing what your company, your department or even your team has to do
- **a target group** – young people, the discerning consumer, people in Scotland, pizza lovers
- **a big summarising idea** – to have access to everyday foods, to be able to visit national parks, to be able to buy clothes in a relaxed family–friendly setting, etc.
- **an implication** – to improve educational access, to ensure that young people can enjoy online entertainment, to help families stretch their budget further.

Some examples of good missions

Have a look at these missions from some big, important companies. Which do you like? Which meet our stress tests above?

eBay:

'At eBay, our mission is to provide a global online marketplace where practically anyone can trade practically anything, enabling economic opportunity around the world.'

Google:

'Organize the world's information and make it universally accessible and useful.'

Save the Children:

'Our mission is to help promote a world in which every child attains the right to survival, protection, development and participation.'

Values

In **Step 1** we talked about values as an important boundary on the strategy road. They are beliefs, principles and attitudes that underpin an organisation's work.

Often, however, they are turned into bland one-word statements, such as integrity or equality, which are neither helpful nor meaningful. Whole phrases or sentences are more likely to create clearer guidelines for action, which is what a company's values should do. Look at the table below and see how values can have important implications.

Value	Statement	Implication
Fair trade	We make sure that all our ingredients are acquired in an ethical way	We ensure that we meet the ethical standards our customers prize
Quality	We are committed to the highest quality products and services	We will refuse to compromise on standards
Family friendly	We organise our services to be easy and comfortable for people with children	We will ensure all our staff are aware of the needs of families
Customer-focused	We put the interests of customers at the centre of our business	We prioritise customer concerns over our commercial interests
Independent	We are not part of a large multinational chain but value being small	We will not sell out to a larger conglomerate and will grow organically

What values does your current company or team espouse? Do you see them in action every day? Are there any disconnects?

When values go wrong, it can be serious. At its peak, Enron was an energy, commodities and services company employing nearly 22,000 people. Based in Texas, it was one of the world's largest energy companies and had been named 'most innovative company in America' for six consecutive years by *Fortune* magazine. The culture was praised as a competitive and talent-focused culture where high performers were rewarded and permitted to launch new projects, often without supervision.

In its annual report to shareholders, Enron listed its core values as follows:

'**Communication** – *We have an obligation to communicate.*

Respect – *We treat others as we would like to be treated.*

Integrity – *We work with customers and prospects openly, honestly, and sincerely.*

Excellence – *We are satisfied with nothing less than the very best in everything we do.*'

(Enron, Annual Report, 2000, p. 29)

Despite all this values talk, the company went bust in 2004 with many employees involved in fraud incompetency and deceit. If you want to know more about one of the largest corporate scandals in history, go to: http://en.wikipedia.org/wiki/Enron_scandal.

Competencies

Competencies – the skills, knowledge or abilities we have or need to develop to achieve the strategy – are the other boundary on the strategy road.

Often there is a connection between values and competencies. For example, if an organisation values creativity, it may need to develop a competency in stimulating new ways of thinking and acting among staff.

Some examples of competencies can include:

- **speed:** responding to changing market situations quickly
- **global:** working genuinely across the world and in a cross-cultural way
- **innovative:** responding with new products or services to emerging needs.

Think about the ways in which Amazon's business has developed over the last few years. The competencies it has developed to help it grow have been in:

- **data-led customer relationship management (CRM)** – to ensure that you are presented with good choices based on your previous purchases

- **logistics** – to be able to offer delivery on time and for very different kinds of goods, from food to electrical
- **IT infrastructure** – to offer a data storage service to others – Amazon is a massive owner of server farms
- **eBook publishing** – to be able to offer a different kind of outlet for, and access to, books
- **hardware manufacture** – to allow it to make, as well as sell, phones, eBook readers and even tablet computers.

Without these competencies, Amazon would not have been able to grow and develop – see the following case study.

Case study

Amazon's leadership values

Amazon is an interesting company that has changed significantly since it was founded in 1994 but, in particular, in the past 10 years. (Note that it did not make a profit for almost 10 years from its original business of selling books.)

Amazon's vision is 'to be Earth's most customer-centric company' and, from that, comes its mission,

> *'[a company] where customers can find and discover anything they might want to buy online, and endeavours to offer its customers the lowest possible prices'.*

Complementing the vision and mission, Amazon has values, mostly based around leadership: 'Whether you are an individual contributor or the manager of a large team, you are an Amazon leader. These are our leadership principles and every Amazonian is guided by these principles.'

Here is just a selection:

- **Customer obsession:** leaders start with the customer and work backwards. They work vigorously to earn and keep customer trust. Although leaders pay attention to competitors, they obsess over customers.
- **Ownership:** leaders are owners. They think long term and do not sacrifice long-term value for short-term results. They act

on behalf of the entire company, beyond just their own team. They never say, 'that's not my job'.

- **Invent and simplify:** leaders expect and require innovation and invention from their teams and always find ways to simplify. They are externally aware, look for new ideas from everywhere and are not limited by 'not invented here'. As we do new things, we accept that we may be misunderstood for long periods of time.

- **Are right, a lot:** leaders are right a lot. They have strong business judgement and good instincts.

- **Hire and develop the best:** leaders raise the performance bar with every hire and promotion. They recognise exceptional talent, and willingly move them throughout the organisation. Leaders develop leaders and take seriously their role in coaching.

- **Insist on the highest standards:** leaders have relentlessly high standards – many people may think these standards are unreasonably high. Leaders are continually raising the bar and driving their teams to deliver high-quality products, services and processes. Leaders ensure that defects do not get sent down the line and that problems are fixed so they stay fixed.

- **Think big:** thinking small is a self-fulfilling prophecy. Leaders create and communicate a bold direction that inspires results. They think differently and look around corners for ways to serve customers.

- **Bias for action:** speed matters in business. Many decisions and actions are reversible and do not need extensive study. We value calculated risk taking.

- **Deliver results:** leaders focus on the key inputs for their business and deliver them with the right quality and in a timely fashion. Despite setbacks, they rise to the occasion and never settle.

Think about yourself in the context of these Amazon values and the competencies they assume. How would you do as a leader in Amazon? How many of these qualities do you have and how many do you need to work on?

 **Exercise**

Create a VMVC for your team or department, if they do not have one. Fill in the boxes below and, as you do, consider the questions.

Vision:

- What does success look like? How would you/others recognise it?
- What is the ultimate aim of the group for which you are developing the VMVC?

Mission:

- How do you deliver value or work towards the vision?
- Whose interests do you need to prioritise?

Values:

- What beliefs or values are important to the way you work?
- What would you not do?

Competencies:

- What core abilities does your team or department need to have now?
- What core abilities does your team or department need to have in the future?

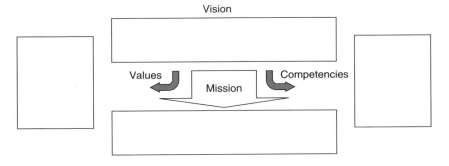

 To see some examples of great – and really terrible – VMVC frameworks, watch our video here:

www.thebusinessgym.net

Call to action

- Are you clear what the key ideas and terms in strategy mean and can you think of good examples of them?

- Are your team's or organisation's vision and mission engaging and clear? Does the vision pass the three tests?

- What is the implication of the values of your company? Do you see senior managers living them? Do *you* live them?

- What current competencies does your organisation have? Which do you think you need to develop to cope with challenges in the next 10 years?

Step 3

Sort out stuff: clarifying the real situation

After reading this step you will be able to:

- Understand how analysis can help inform strategy
- Use the two most common and helpful analysis tools
- Conduct a PEST and SWOT analysis
- Realise the limitations of analysis.

What business are we in (WBAWIN)?

 In order to begin any kind of strategy – crafted or planned – you have to understand where you are now.

It is the same approach as deciding to build your fitness programme around an assessment of your current health and fitness.

There are a number of analysis tools that you can use to help here – common ones include competitor analysis and benchmarking. (We look at some of these in other parts of the book.) And there are some weird acronyms for other models like SCRS (strategy, current state, requirements, solution) and MoSCoW (must have – or else delivery will be a failure; should have – otherwise will have to adopt a workaround; could have – to increase delivery satisfaction; would like to have in the future – but will not have now).

When analysing your situation, you should think about your overall business context. To use a sporting analogy – what sport are you playing and what league are you in? The rules are different for each sport. In football, it makes a big difference if you are playing in the Scottish First Division or the Champions League – most obviously in terms of the economics. (Think how it affects the cost of a top player and how much you can earn from merchandise.) So, back in your own world, what business are you in – healthy snacks or junk food, computer hardware or consumer electronics? And what business league is your company playing in – local, national, international or even global? Do you work business to business or business to consumer?

 **Exercise**

Take a minute to consider what business you are in. Describe it as simply as you can and then what you might want to change. If you are in an HR team, should you be in the talent development business rather than the sorting-out-contracts-and-performance-problems business, as HR people often feel they are in? Interestingly, IBM has replaced its HR department with a change department – arguing that the job is really about helping staff deal with change.

At a company level, what do you see happening? Is the company trying to be more or less national or international? Is it trying to be in a different core area or stay the same? So, Innocent, the fruit drinks company, moved into the food business with vegetable and noodle pots and then, in 2015, moved back out again.

As you decide WBAWIN, consider these two questions:

1. What evidence do you have for this analysis? For example, who are your competitors?

2. What is distinctive about this league? How might it change? What might that mean for you?

Harvard Business School 101: PEST and SWOT

There are two tools most often used to establish a team's or company's current position – PEST and SWOT analysis. We have people saying these are over used but, in our experience, these are just the best and simplest tools for the job. If you need more convincing, on day 1 at Harvard, on your Executive MBA course, you will be introduced to these two key frameworks. (PEST was actually invented at Harvard by Michael Porter and SWOT at Stanford by Albert Humphrey.) The good news is you are probably familiar with them. But in this step we want to make sure you do them systematically rather than in a slightly desultory way, as often happens.

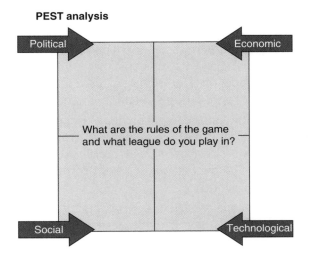

PEST analysis

Political

Economic

What are the rules of the game and what league do you play in?

Social

Technological

SWOT analysis

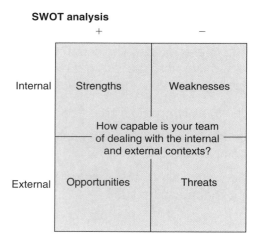

PEST - how to work out the rules

PEST stands for political, economic, social and technological. You use this analysis to establish the main forces at play in the business context in which you and your competitors operate. Going back to our sporting analogy, it is the rules of the game – the things that are the case and the things that you cannot change, but you may need to adapt to as you plot your strategy. (So, if you want to play football, each half lasts 45 minutes and there are 11 people on each side. Those are the rules and you have to play by them.)

In a business context, you are looking at answering the following questions:

- **Political:** what legal framework shapes your industry? Is there a piece of legislation – e.g. on consumer rights – that will affect you? How are your regulators changing, e.g. local council planning permissions? Is your business impacted nationally or locally?

- **Economic:** how is your sector doing economically overall? Is there anything that you know is affecting everyone's performance – such as lack of credit or finance? What is the prognosis? How are employment rates or wages overall affecting your work?

- **Social:** what social factors are in play? Is the ageing population having an effect? Are you fashionable or uncool as a business?

Is public opinion for or against your industry? (Something that might affect you if you are in tobacco or pharmaceuticals, for example.)

- **Technological:** what significant changes are happening that could affect you and your competitors? Are there new payment methods, such as smartphones? Are any emerging technologies affecting you – making things cheaper, easier to make, more accessible?

You will be sure to find lots of variants on PEST as you undertake your strategy gym workout – normally with letters added on to signify additional issues, such as environmental, ethics, regulatory, etc. Some common variants are PESTEL or PESTLE, STEEPLE, STEEPLED and even STEER.

 If you are keen to explore these alternatives, there is a useful Wikipedia article on them all at:

http://en.wikipedia.org/wiki/PEST_analysis

We are going to encourage you to stay mainstream and work with PEST – but, of course, to consider within PEST issues such as ethics, the environment, etc.

Why use analysis - and why not

PEST analysis and other analysis tools have a number of uses:

- To clarify what game you want to play (sometimes, of course, you have to change the game you are playing – see pivoting in **Challenge 4**).
- As a way of assessing what league you are in – local, regional, national or international – and what league you would like to be in.
- As part of a process of working out the likely future forces – the drivers (see **Step 4**) – that you have to deal with in your plan.
- In order to establish what new competencies you may have to develop in order to tackle any emerging situation. (Think back to **Step 1**.)

Be aware, though, that there are downsides to analysis:

- It can be an alluring and time-consuming process – while the world changes fast, you seek even more data looking for the perfect information, the right answer.
- Make sure you avoid the complementary challenge: what is called 'paralysis by analysis' – having so much data that it freezes action.

Tate Gallery: multi-business, multi-league

We have worked a lot with the great team at Tate Gallery over the years. And one part of that work has involved trying to establish the many different dimensions of Tate.

- **Geography:** Tate Modern is an international player, Tate Britain a national one, and the St Ives and Liverpool variants a mix of national and regional. This makes a big difference, for example, to who they appeal to for sponsorship funds and who the visitors are.
- **Core business:** well, of course, they are all art galleries. But they are also in the merchandise business, the catering business, the conservation business, the education business and even the tourism business. For each of these businesses, there are different demographic, financial and legal/political constraints.

Working on a strategy plan for Tate St Ives we had to create PEST analysis that reflected each of these dimensions. PEST should reflect this complexity.

PEST is useful in that it forces you to think about the big picture in which you operate. But it is also useful to generate scenarios – possible future situations over the strategic horizon – that you might need to deal with. See **Step 5** on futurology for how to do this.

Case study

InsureCo PEST example

You are in the marketing department of InsureCo – a small local company providing household insurance through your high-street retail outlet. With your colleagues you might come up with the following simple PEST:

P	E
• very detailed legislation: restricts our offer • Data Protection Act makes marketing difficult • regulator insisting on more documentation	• online competition makes people very price sensitive • margins very low, so profitability is a challenge • banks offering basic insurance as part of accounts
S	T
• consumers want to combine insurances – one-stop shop • high fraud level – seen as victimless crime • people prefer online browsing	• use of credit cards increasing: we have to meet 2.5% merchanting fee • local radio advertising inexpensive and easy • improved marketing databases make targeting easier

Checklist for a PEST

Use the questions below as a way of beginning a checklist for a PEST analysis.

Political	Economic
• What legislation does or will impact on you? • What activities are allowed or not allowed by your values or by regulators?	• What is happening to sources of growth finance – how does that affect investment? • How is demand for your service, product or offering changing?

Political	Economic
• What legal and ethical standards must you meet?	• Is there pressure for cost cutting in response to competition/consumers?
Social	Technological
• Is your brand hot or not and how does that impact on customer demand? • Is the size of your target market increasing or decreasing? • Are customers changing in terms of gender, demography, income, etc.?	• How does social media impact on production or service delivery? • Is technology making a difference in your industry? • Do changes in technology mean a rise or fall in demand for your services?

What game are you playing and what league are you in?

SWOT: how to assess your team and its chances for success

If the PEST analysis offers you a guide to the context in which you and your competitors have to operate, a SWOT analysis identifies the specific situation of your organisation and its ability to compete. This normally is drawn up as a 2×2 matrix, placing positive and negative on one axis and internal and external on another (see table on page 37). Each of the quadrants is then labelled: strengths, weaknesses, opportunities and threats.

- **Strengths:** are the specific, *positive* internal advantages you have – a good brand, comprehensive training, great IT, useful management information/insight, clear policy guidelines, an effective CEO, positive cash flow, etc.
- **Weaknesses:** are the specific, *negative* internal difficulties you have – undertrained colleagues, high staff turnover, weak senior management, lack of definite marketing strategy, weak sales stream, poor quality control, etc.
- **Opportunities:** are the specific, *positive* external chances you have to improve – a new source of capital, a big contract

to be won, access to a potentially better building, a piece of legislation that makes business easier, a link up with a big supplier, etc.

- **Threats:** are the specific *negative* external circumstances that could damage the organisation – legal action from a failure to comply with legislation, a rival setting up and taking share, a potentially damaging press campaign, some change in technology that threatens your business model, etc.

SWOT combines *internal* and *external* + *positive* and *negative* in a simple powerful matrix. Below are some checklist questions for you to use.

Strengths	Weaknesses
<ul><li>How effective is your leadership – board and senior managers?</li><li>How effective and aligned are staff? Is morale high?</li><li>How well do you work with partners and suppliers?</li><li>Is your brand recognised and valued by customers?</li><li>Is the quality of your service or product good?</li><li>Is your marketing and customer service effective?</li><li>Do you have a significant capital or investment budget?</li></ul>	<ul><li>How ineffective is leadership – board and senior managers?</li><li>Are staff unaligned or ineffective? Is morale low?</li><li>Do you have weak partners/suppliers or poor relationships?</li><li>Is your brand unrecognised or not valued by customers?</li><li>Is the quality of your service or product uneven?</li><li>Is your marketing and customer service ineffective?</li><li>Do you have limited capital or no investment budget?</li></ul>
Opportunities	Threats
<ul><li>Are existing customers growing or new ones appearing?</li><li>Is a new technology about to become available that will make it easier to deliver your offering?</li></ul>	<ul><li>Are customers growing or new ones shrinking or disappearing?</li><li>Does a competitor have a new technology, making it easier/cheaper to deliver their offering?</li></ul>

Opportunities	Threats
• Is a competitor weak or losing market share? • Are there opportunities for mergers or partnerships?	• Is an effective competitor about to appear or grow? • Are competitors merging or forming partnerships?

 **Exercise**

Now assess your company, department or team. Be honest and candid. Use the checklist above to help complete the matrix.

Strengths	Weaknesses
Opportunities	Threats

 To see an example of how PEST and SWOT link, see our video here:

www.thebusinessgym.net

 **Exercise**

Imagine you are a member of the new management team in a well-established network of five leisure centres in town. You are not very profitable and want to improve, but you have only limited opportunity to invest in order to attract more profitable business. What should you do? Before deciding where to focus time and money, you need to scope out all the issues – where are the issues to tackle?

S	W
• good track record of marketing to young people • five leisure centres with high membership and user levels • new ambitious management team	• poorly paid and possibly demotivated trainers • weak management information – so unclear on most profitable areas • limited capital for expansion and upgrading
O	T
• market research says customers keen to sign up if quality offering • new government grant scheme for employee customer care training • good credit deals for new equipment	• Leisurama PLC set up high-end centre in town and takes customers • economic downturn means customers cancel memberships • local newspaper gives centres bad write-up

Call to action

Once you have completed your SWOT and PEST analyses, you should be able to:

- identify the big issues that your organisation, department or team is facing: what is fixed and represents the rules of the game?

- establish how good your team is: are they able to tackle the issues that might arise?

It is also worth:

- getting someone else to check out your ideas – you may be blindsided to possible positives and negatives

- checking for platitudes – for example, have you really got a good team? It is tempting to say so, but is it really the case?

Step 4

Do not sweat the small stuff: dealing with what is important

After reading this step you will be able to:

- Avoid sweating the small stuff, addressing issues that are not strategic
- Avoid some of the problems with over-analysing situations
- Prioritise main issues to address – the key drivers
- Develop insights from your analysis
- Avoid focusing on irrelevant or unimportant issues.

What should I worry about?

Strategy is not just about decisive action (though it ends up being about that). It needs to be the *right* action. And, to take the right action, you need to address the right issue or issues. There are a number of ways to make sure you tackle the right issues. In this step we explore three of the techniques most commonly used. Choose the one that fits with your confidence level and how mission critical getting the strategy right is.

Others in the team may be more experienced than you – that does not mean they cannot make mistakes or miss out on some key issues. The techniques outlined below are all designed so that you can use them to ask the right questions – then use others to help frame choices.

Technique 1: Delphic model

The simplest technique to find out key issues to address is the Delphic model. In this you simply identify a group of, perhaps, 6–10 senior individuals or external experts and ask them to write down their responses to one or more questions – at the simplest, 'what are the most pressing issues we need to address in the next 3–5 years?' Each of the senior people/experts initially is asked to respond individually without consultation – so you avoid groupthink. You then share the responses and ask the Delphic group to comment on each other's points of view.

Finally, you seek consensus on the key issues. The consensus represents the best guess of the Delphic team.

- **Key advantage:** you have sought the opinion of the best people available and their thoughts are probably wise.
- **Key disadvantage:** experts can tend to reinforce the status quo, so you may not get radical advice. Therefore, choose some outsiders.

Note also that senior managers and experts often like to be asked for their opinion – it makes them feel important. So, by using Delphic techniques, you can make some important contacts that will help you later in your career and you can look smart by using other people's opinions.

Technique 2: MoSCoW method

MoSCoW is a simple technique, similar to the Delphic approach. In this case, you reach out and seek the views of key stakeholders on the relative importance of significant issues. Following a brainstorm of possible issues, you then prioritise them, based on the capital letters in the acronym.

M	**Must:** is an issue that has to be addressed absolutely directly in the strategy if it is to be considered a success. All of the must issues have to be dealt with or the strategy will be a failure.
S	**Should:** is a high-impact issue that should be addressed, if it is possible. They are as important as musts, but are not as time-critical. If dealt with in the strategy, note that there should be an explanation on how it will be dealt with.
C	**Could:** refers to something that it is desirable to address in the strategy, but not necessary. These should be addressed, if they do not entail risk or significant strategic resources.
W	**Will not:** is a cluster of issues that have been examined and are not mission-critical at all. The strategy should consciously put these to one side, having assessed them.

Technique 3: creating drivers - turning data into insight

Let us focus now on a technique we use most commonly. So, as you may remember in **Step 2**, we looked at how to systematically *analyse* the strategic situation you are in – ensuring that you identify all the possible issues you need to consider.

 Analysis is essential to making any kind of progress.

Unfortunately, though, this kind of thorough analysis can itself cause some challenges. For example, you can:

- spend too long collecting data and information, and miss an opportunity

- collect irrelevant information – and get side-tracked
- have so much information that it is hard to make sense of it.

The secret is to take the data you have collected, identify the key issues you need to address and turn them into bits of insight that we call strategic drivers. Identifying drivers is not easy and may take some time. But it is worth the investment to make sure you end up tackling the right issues.

Like strategy itself, there is no common definition of a driver. A driver in our approach is in two parts:

- a fact or piece of data
- the implication of that fact.

It is important to stress that a driver is not a solution and that there can be different implications from a single piece of data. By keeping this in mind, you can be sure you do not jump to the wrong conclusion straight away. For example:

The fact	The possible implications A or B
We are losing market share to competitors	A. We need to identify what our competitors are doing and match it
We are losing market share to competitors	B. We need to do something different to distinguish ourselves from our competitors

So, the same bit of data can have two very different implications. Here is another example:

The fact	The possible implications A or B
Our salary bill is 20 per cent higher than our competitors'	A. We need to find a way to reduce salaries so that we can compete on a level playing field
Our salary bill is 20 per cent higher than our competitors'	B. If our staff are worth more since they are more experienced, can we adjust prices to meet costs?

There are a number of ways that you can choose to ensure the quality of your output or implication. The easiest way is simply to ask different groups to think about the same piece of data and see how they process it differently. (So, you can combine this with the Delphic approach above.)

How to identify key issues: strategic drivers

You probably need two main clusters of drivers: internal and external. Internal drivers cover issues to do with internal capacities. External ones concern the impact of competitors, customers or the general context. It is helpful to aim to end up with five to seven drivers in each category. That number should ensure you are dealing only with the major issues.

There are several steps towards identifying drivers and it is easiest when done in a group. You may want to call together colleagues or offer to facilitate a senior group.

1. First, gather together all your data from **Step 2** in one place. Allow people to read it, ideally in twos or threes, so you get a diversity of opinion on relative importance. Make it clear they are meant to be looking at issues to be addressed – not coming up with solutions.

2. Ask the small groups to write what they think of as a key piece of data or information on a sticky note. Do not worry if they disagree about whether it is important, but do make sure they stick to the rule about writing down facts, figures or data.

3. Put all the sticky notes up on a wall organised, first, by where they came from – so, in the figure below, you can see it is done by PEST and SWOT. You could also include data from competitor analysis, financial trends, etc.

4. Put up your vision and mission on the wall. And then use the VMVC to prioritise – by votes or acclamation – how important these bits of data are, or will be, in the strategic horizon. Prioritise using A (very important), B (quite important), C (relatively important). Write these letters on the sticky notes.

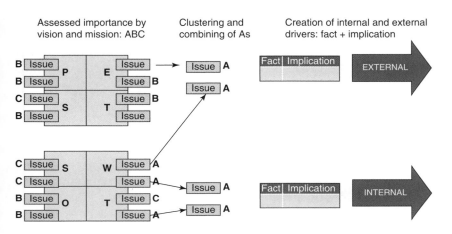

Assessed importance by vision and mission: ABC | Clustering and combining of As | Creation of internal and external drivers: fact + implication

5. OK, that is the easy bit. Now put aside the Bs and Cs. (You decided they were not important, so stick with that.) But keep them – views can change, as can situations.

6. Now cluster your As. Begin by dividing them into what you think are internal and external issues. Use the checklist in the following table to help decide where a piece of data should go. If necessary, make copies of the sticky notes so they can go in more than one place.

7. Next, cluster the sticky notes into themes or topics. These themes should arise from the clustering but, typically, might also involve some of the issues in the following table:

Internal driver checklist	External driver checklist
Staff morale	Changes in customer demographics
Staff recruitment/retention	Competition
Culture	Changes in customer needs
Quality	Partnerships and suppliers
Internal innovation	Price or cost sensitivity
Leadership	External innovation
Capital to use	Legislation
Marketing	Changes in interest rates

8. Once you have organised the sticky notes into clusters, write beside each one a possible implication (see examples earlier). You may have to put up some different implications. So 'competitors have cut their prices by 20 per cent' is a fact. But this fact could have different implications: 'we need to cut our prices, too' or 'we need to differentiate our proposition and make it clearly premium'.

9. *Voilà!* You have identified the key drivers for the business, for your department or for your team. But, health warning! *Things can change.* You may need to revisit the analysis and the drivers on a regular basis to check they are still relevant *and* important. And some of those Bs or Cs can become As in time.

Galileo: and the problem of identifying the key issue

In the 16th century, Galileo got into a lot of trouble with the Catholic Church for challenging the accepted thinking that the sun went round the earth.

He simply used the data that existed, but drew a completely different (and accurate) implication from it that the earth went round the sun.

 Moral: do not expect your thinking to be welcomed by everyone, even if it is based on data.

 To see a practical example of how drivers are formed from analyses, see our video here:

www.thebusinessgym.net

Case study

Residential Care Co

We worked with a residential care company, Bield, which offered sheltered housing in Edinburgh to people with special needs and older residents.

The company had noticed some key changes in its market that made it want to develop a new strategic plan. Some of the changes Bield noticed were:

- more big contracts being offered by local authorities to a smaller number of agencies through very cut-throat competitive tendering

- less demand for special needs accommodation, but much more demand for specialised dementia care

- a much higher wage bill than its competitors – partly as a result of success in retaining staff who then looked for annual salary rises

- competitors were recruiting cheaper staff internationally, especially from Eastern Europe, who were highly skilled but cheaper.

The company spotted these issues quickly, but it wanted to go deeper. So it undertook a number of analyses: PEST, SWOT, customer satisfaction survey, staff satisfaction survey, benchmarking against other agencies, competitor analysis, stakeholder consultation and demographic analysis.

Bield collected the data and divided it up into discrete chunks of information. As in the model above these were transferred to sticky notes and put up on a wall.

As a group, the management team then undertook the ABC prioritisation process, added implications, dividing them up into internal and external drivers.

External drivers

External driver fact	Driver implication
• Public funding allocations are changing and reducing • Future government budgets suggest a reduction in care support and emphasis on self-reliance	Reduced public funding means we have to look at new sources of support
• Our success rate for tenders is low and this is an important core skill • We have limited resources committed to winning tenders	The competitive context – for market share, for private and public funds, for tenders – means 'more for less' and cost competition
• Government statistics and demographics plus our tenant and service data signal emerging trends • Over 85s will increase 38% in 10 years and there is no real provision for this group established at scale	The growth in the older population will change the ways we provide services and the kinds of services we provide
• Government statistics indicate changing demographics for older people • Stakeholder and partner experience suggests different needs emerging	The significant growth in dementia – a function of a growing older population – will change the services people need and that we have to provide
• Feedback from customers/beneficiaries is that we do a good job • Market trends and data say there are changing perceptions of quality and acceptability	Our customers have changing aspirations in terms of what they want – from accommodation type to service levels. We need to assess and address these

External driver fact	Driver implication
• Government policy is changing and there is uncertainty about personalisation agenda • In Scotland and further afield there may be an impending change in government	Government policies are changing – as the government may – and we need to stay abreast of these changes

Internal drivers

Internal driver fact	Driver implication
• Consultations and structural reviews suggest some frustration among staff and stakeholders • We struggle to work in a joined-up way and that will become increasingly important	We seem to duplicate effort – and this may make us less competitive and unintegrated, and so less efficient
• Our governance and committee structures are old-fashioned and may not be fit for purpose • Customer, staff and partner feedback suggests many people are not clear on what we do	We sometimes seem to have an inability to respond to change effectively and we need to be faster
• Customer trends show greater demand for high quality service • We work in an increasingly competitive market place – many private providers and other HAs entering	To secure customer loyalty in the face of growing competition we need to maintain a high level of customer satisfaction

Internal driver fact	Driver implication
• Staff consultations suggest we do not always communicate effectively • Existing departmental structures have been in place for some time	We operate in departmental and geographical silos — and this may mean information and ideas are not shared easily, and we miss opportunities
• Our staff retention means we have an ageing and expensive workforce • Staff survey indicates areas of concern in terms of morale – few promotion opportunities	If Bield is to deliver outstanding customer service it needs to be the Employer of Choice to attract new staff and retain key staff
• Our governance structures – developed when Bield was much smaller – do not seem appropriate • Other agencies are working in a more entrepreneurial way – and growing	Our governance, leadership and management structures need to be flexible and able to compete effectively in a fast-changing market

 **Exercise**

Review the PEST and SWOT you completed in **Step 3** for your team, department or organisation. Identify as many issues as possible with specific bits of data attached and put them beside your VMVC. Then, as described above, ABC each of the issues in terms of your vision and mission. Move all the As together and look for those vital few clusters. Use the checklist above to help. Then put them into a table, like the one below.

External facts from analysis	Likely implication
Internal facts from analysis	Likely implication

Once you have done this, you will have a fairly solid set of drivers. The next phase is to decide how to tackle these drivers. The rest of the book will help you with this.

Engaging lots of people ... or a few?

Several times we have created a simple engagement format in the online survey software Survey Monkey to allow widely distributed organisations to involve many hundreds, or even thousands, of staff and managers in deciding what the key drivers should be from a range of identified issues.

We have done this with a multinational organisation spread across 160 countries, asking every small and large branch to contribute. The result was a fully involved group of almost 6,000 managers and staff who really engaged with the issues. They were then much more ready to accept the proposed solutions in the strategic plan.

Call to action

- Can you help identify and prioritise the big issues that your organisation, department or team is facing?

- What techniques should you use to identify the big issues? What will have most credibility?

- Is it clear to you that you have identified all the issues that need to be addressed? Are there any that might be missing?

- Who could you turn to, to check that these are the key issues? Can you identify external individuals with independent minds to help?

- Can you separate the facts or data from the implication? Together, they form the driver, but make sure you sense-check the implication.

- Who can you turn to and check out whether your opinion is accurate or backed up by evidence?

Step 5

Imagine possibilities: thinking like a futurologist

After reading this step you will be able to:

- Understand how to think imaginatively about the future
- Explain the difference between trends analysis and scenarios
- Appreciate the potential use of a scenario approach
- Develop some scenarios for your own work.

The problem with prediction

Strategy is about the future. If only it was possible to plan the future with any real degree of certainty, business – and life – would be much easier. In truth, the new reality often can be stranger than we imagine and a good strategy should take this possibility into account. (See **Skill 7** on black swans for really weird stuff.)

As a result of this, the principles of futurology, or scenario planning, are becoming increasingly popular and useful for anyone developing a strategy in what seems destined to remain an uncertain and fast-changing world. A well-organised scenario planning session will help you to avoid the dreaded paralysis by analysis mentioned in **Step 3** and it will allow you to contribute some of your fresh thinking about the future. (Sometimes, senior managers find new thinking most acceptable from younger or more junior colleagues. Seize the chance to share your ideas and encourage others to come up with their radical ideas.)

Even the experts get it wrong

History is littered with cases of the leading experts getting the future wrong. Here are some famous examples:

'Make no mistake, this weapon will change absolutely nothing.'

General Haig, UK Commander,
on the first use of the machine gun in 1914

'I think there is a world market for maybe five computers.'

Tom Watson, CEO IBM, on demand for computers in 1943

'We don't like their sound, and guitar music is on the way out.'

Decca Recording Co., rejecting The Beatles in 1962

'It's a bad joke that won't last. Not with winter coming.'

Coco Chanel on the miniskirt in 1966

'640K ought to be enough for anybody.'

Bill Gates, on the need for computer memory in 1981

'You'll never make any money out of children's books.'

Barry Cunningham, editor at Bloomsbury Books,
to J. K. Rowling in 1996

Scenario planning is now regularly used by many of the largest companies worldwide, including Shell, Walmart, British Telecom, Accenture and even Disney. The commercial originator was Shell, which developed a number of scenarios in the 1990s to identify what its future challenges might be. It is important to say that most of the scenarios it created did not happen – but a number did. So, for example, Shell predicted the first Gulf War and the effect it would have on oil prices, and, as a result, had plans to deal with this. Key learning is that scenarios are about possibilities.

Let us be clear. Scenarios are not trends or predictions extrapolating out from the past to the future – though these are the basis of most strategic thinking. In scenario planning, you begin by creating a limited number of possible outcomes and then work out how likely this is to happen and what you would do if that situation – scenario – developed. It is the difference between what is called strategic hindsight and strategic foresight.

The figures and table below illustrate this essential difference.

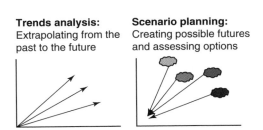

Trends analysis:
Extrapolating from the past to the future

Scenario planning:
Creating possible futures and assessing options

This fundamental difference is important since, in one case, you start from what you know and work out towards the future. And, in the second, you begin from what might be possible and work back to what you know. The following table expands on this distinction:

	Conventional planning	Scenario planning
Focus	Exploring how current trends might extrapolate out and how strategy would need to align or adjust	Imagining possible futures and how strategy would need to change or transform
Advantages	• Well-established models to create this • What most people do and is safe(ish) • Emphasises business as – almost – usual	• Emerging models available, which energise thinking • May allow real insights and unlock creativity • Allows for business outside the box
Disadvantages	• May stop you identifying discontinuous change • Can encourage blindsiding – missing stuff – or fixed thinking • May put energy into lost causes rather than give up	• Models to create this are not as well known • Few companies do it systematically • May absorb energy on unlikely possibilities

Why use scenario planning?

There are a number of reasons to try scenario planning:

- It is a collaborative approach, encouraging the interaction of ideas from a range of people.
- It reframes questions and assumptions, which should help generate ideas across teams, disciplines and departments, rather than recycling old ones.
- Unlike forecasting, scenarios are not based on consensus, so differences and challenges are welcome – dissent has an impact and value!

- The story format of scenarios ensures qualitative and quantitative elements are included, so ideas are not excluded just because they cannot be measured.

- By building sets of scenarios, you assemble several different versions of the future in parallel – so possibilities and options are created, *not* certain outcomes.

How to develop a scenario

There are five key stages to develop scenarios and then plan your response to them:

Stage 1: Clarify the challenge

The starting point for scenario planning is, normally, identifying some major uncertainty. For example, you may be concerned that some radical technological change might happen – perhaps you produce petrol cars and are wondering whether electric ones will take over. Or you sell oil-fired heaters and you want to know what the impact of really cheap alternative energy would be. Or, if you are making a scenario for your team, what would happen if your work was outsourced to India?

One way to develop a radical option is to think of your greatest fear or greatest hope. (See Dreams and Nightmares in the exercise below.)

Stage 2: Analyse the current situation

Scenario building is, initially, a creative process, using imagination to create possibilities. You can stimulate these possibilities by looking through:

- material from magazines to identify consumer/user changes
- ideas from think tanks – especially radical ones
- research papers that propose technology changes.

Stage 3: Identify the key dimensions

Normally, you develop some dimensions on which to plot the scenarios. Classic dimensions are likely/unlikely and high impact/

low impact. But there are other dimensions you might consider, such as local/international, positive/negative, formal/informal, children/adults, urban/rural and profitable/unprofitable. This structure – using two sets of opposites – allows you to create axes like the ones on page 59.

Stage 4: Generate scenarios

Scenarios should be more than writing down one simple outcome. If you were in the language school business, you might think of scenarios arising from the invention of instant and accurate language translation software. Some scenarios are likely to have an impact well beyond your school and could affect holiday making, advertising and even dating websites.

In this step you should also identify how likely or unlikely the scenario is. Some of the best scenarios are provocative and maybe even improbable.

Stage 5: Develop narratives

Normally, these basic scenarios are then developed into narratives. These are small stories, which explore through the lives of individuals or groups what this change might mean.

So, for the instant language translation, you could explore what the development of such software might mean for:

- publishers of dictionaries
- professional translators
- international lawyers
- people who run holiday companies/holiday makers
- people looking to move overseas in search of employment.

 **Exercise**

Creating scenarios can be a long and detailed process. If you want to do it fast, then here is a quick alternative way.

Dreams

Get a small group of colleagues – and maybe even some outsiders – to write down their three wishes about the business. If they had an Aladdin-style magic lamp, what would they wish for that would make a radical difference in the business? (A never-ending battery, a bin that sorts its own recycling, an anti-retroviral that adapts to match the HIV virus?) Encourage them to be as wild and free as possible. The only rule is that they believe it would make a radical difference to the business.

Nightmares

Now get people to think about their worst nightmares. What could happen that would be a nightmare for the agency? An anti-Aladdin's lamp, if you like. A nightmare could be the same as a wish, depending on what business you are in. It could be high-fat food, such as burgers, is legally banned (McDonald's), cheap instant language translation becomes a reality (language schools), a never-stain material is discovered (dry cleaners).

Now place these dream and nightmare possibilities on two dimensions, *likely to happen* and *scale of impact,* as shown in the following figure.

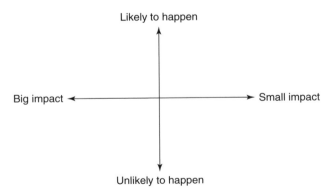

Focus now on the scenarios on the big impact side of the diagram. Do not worry about likely to happen or unlikely at the moment. You have already divided them into positive and negative using the nightmare and dream division. From this starting point you need to develop a response for each scenario. You can do that in a table:

Positive – dream – scenarios	Action	Negative – nightmare – scenarios	Action
How can we increase the likelihood?		How can we decrease the likelihood?	
How likely is it to happen?		How likely is it to happen?	
What, specifically, would we do in response?		What, specifically, would we do in response?	
What implications would it have? Any negative implications?		What implications would it have? Any positive implications?	

It is very tempting to focus on the likely to happen scenarios. But, remember, it is worth considering the very unlikely, but very high impact, scenarios at least. With these, you have to ask yourself an additional set of questions:

- Why do you believe it is so unlikely to happen? Are you sure?
- In what circumstances might it happen?
- What bad things would it mean for your business?
- Are there any positive possible outcomes?

The purpose in doing this is to stretch your thinking and make sure you are not dismissing possibilities too soon – or properly thinking through how disruptive the unlikely outcome might be. See **Skills 3, 7** and **9** for more on this issue.

Case study

The London bombings 7/7

One practical example from our own work might help show the value of scenarios.

In 2007, just weeks before the London terrorist bombings of 7/7, we were hired by the Mayor's Office to work alongside the British Red Cross (BRC) to conduct a scenario planning exercise into how the City would raise and distribute money for victims in a disaster. (Separate plans were in place for the medical response and dealing with damage to infrastructure.) Working with the BRC and others, we created a number of scenarios:

- a sudden flood
- a fire or earthquake
- a terrorist attack
- a plane or train crash.

We then assessed the implications of these scenarios in terms of fundraising and fund distribution to victims. A starting point was to work alongside the The International Federation of Red Cross and Red Cross Societies internationally to study the fundraising work that had happened after the 9/11 attacks and Bali bombings, as well as other disasters. Sadly, as we now know, there had been little advance planning for those improbable situations.

From this data, we created a number of story narratives that we could use to plan. Some of these were deliberately extreme, for example 20,000 people killed at a football match in the confusion following a bomb. In another, we looked at 10 members of the UK cabinet being injured after the Thames flooded. Remember, we were looking at the implications for the sums that might be raised and how these sums should be distributed. (One important lesson from 9/11, for example, was that giving out the money in a way that was seen as equitable and proper was much more difficult than raising it.) We also needed to look at issues where the learning was less obvious, such as how many telephone lines would be needed to cope with 2,000/5,000/10,000 calls a minute to donation lines. And how many people would give online, versus how many would send cheques, versus how many would turn up at banks with cash.

Sadly, our work was put into practice all too soon when the bombers struck, literally weeks after we had started the project.

Even the limited scenarios work we had done until then, and the planning associated with it, proved invaluable as a massive fundraising, and then funds distribution, campaign was set up.

The learning from our work has now been written up with the British Red Cross and shared around the world.

 To hear Bernard Ross talking about scenario planning for the London Bombings of 2007 go to:

www.thebusinessgym.net

Call to action

- How did your team or business arrive at the current situation? What were the turning points in the past? Did anyone spot them in advance? What are the lessons?

- What legacy would you like to leave? What three wishes would you like to have, if you could?

- If you had the chance, what questions would you ask of an oracle about the future? How far into the future would you like to see?

- What would be a very bad outcome for your business or team? What events could lead to such an outcome?

Step 6

Know your enemy: assessing the competition

After reading this step you will be able to:

- Understand who the competition is – and how/where they compete
- Spot some weird or unexpected competition
- Appreciate why it is important to assess the competition
- Identify how to compete effectively.

Life would be much simpler if all you had to worry about was your company and your customers. But you also need to think about the competition. Worse still, your competitors may not be the obvious rivals.

 Think about who is going for the same customers and needs rather than who simply appears to be in the same business as you.

Coca-Cola, for example, sees water as a rival for 'stomach share' rather than simply competing against Pepsi or other sodas for the fizzy drink market.

 **Exercise**

Begin by making a list of agencies who you think of as being your rivals. Are they a strong (A), medium (B) or weak (C) competitor? Then think about how they compete – across all of your offerings, one customer/consumer segment or many?

Competitor	A, B, C?	Which customers/consumers do they compete for?

Who is the competition – and how do they compete?

As already indicated, the competition is not always obvious. So, if you run a business airline, is the competition only other business airlines? Or is it actually email? Or Skype?

Who you see as the competition will dictate your competitive strategy.

 You might enjoy this blog from Harvard:

https://hbr.org/2015/05/the-first-question-to-ask-of-any-strategy?

Case study

Language school

You need to be careful not to be blindsided by simplistic discussions about what business you are in. If you are in the business of selling foreign language DVDs, you might think the competition is other people selling language DVDs. But, if you define the customer offering as 'acquiring a foreign language', then the competition could be:

- language schools that combine holidays with language schools
- books
- online courses
- personal language tutors
- schools/educational agencies running adult learning classes.

For each of these, the way you respond could be slightly different. Think about how your competition strategy would vary.

Develop competitive advantage

Think about your main competitors. How can you distinguish your company from them? What are your sources of competitive advantage?

- **Brand:** how do people feel about your offering/products/ service or company?
- **Value:** are you seen as providing base value, like Aldi, or high value, like Tiffany?
- **Values:** do your values themselves help – e.g. fairtrade, customer-orientated?

- **Service:** does your service distinguish you – more stock, knowledgeable staff?
- **Reach:** do you have more branches, affiliates or channels than your rivals?

If you are not different from your competitor, you have no competitive advantage and you become a commodity and indistinguishable from others.

 **Exercise**

Which of these competitive advantages do you have or might you want to acquire?

Main competitors	How are we distinct from them?	How might we develop a distinction from them?

 To find out about different ways of creating competitive advantage, watch Clare Segal discuss Kotler's Egg at:

www.thebusinessgym.net

Where is the competition?

When you are thinking about your competitors, you may want to think about the way in which you compete, or the level at which you compete, as well as who you compete with. The following figure illustrates the main levels you should consider.

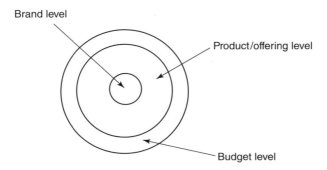

Almost certainly, you have to compete with others for customers at a number of levels. Let us look at what these levels might mean.

- **Brand:** here you are compared directly with a company seen as 'doing the same thing', e.g. Heinz or Crosse & Blackwell baked beans and Santander or Barclays Bank. In these cases, the product or offering is basically the same, the differentiator might simply be brand – how people feel about or perceive your product, offering or company.

- **Offering:** here you are compared to an offering that is the same. If you think of beans as being a quick and cheap snack, you might compare them with other quick and cheap snacks, such as eggs. Both are easy to prepare and provide reasonable nutrition.

- **Budget:** here you compete for a specific budget category where there is, fundamentally, a different kind of choice for the customer, e.g. choosing to go to the cinema or buy a self-help book. Both might cost about the same, but they come from different budgets – entertainment versus education, in the same way a big purchase item might involve choosing whether to refurbish the kitchen or go on a cruise. Competition here is much more radical.

Once you have decided at which level you compete, you can then decide how you should compete. Revisit the exercise above and see if this helps you add ideas.

To compete or not?

We cannot write a chapter about competition without mentioning Michael Porter. You should be familiar with his name and ideas to hold your own in a strategic discussion. At one point, Porter was the hottest – and most expensive! – management consultant in the world. He produced a number of big ideas but, perhaps, his most famous is the Five Forces Model. Essentially, this is a framework that allows you – at an organisational or business units level – to:

- work out the dynamics in any market or area of activity
- establish what your best competitive position is
- decide if you can successfully enter a market
- work out who you need to partner with in any enterprise
- identify what the implications are of exiting a market.

Porter says you can decide what to do in terms of market position by assessing five key forces:

- **New entrants:** are there many potential new entrants keen to get into this market – or are there barriers like a licence to entry?
- **Buyer's power:** can buyers – from customers to retailers – negotiate about price/availability level and so put you under pressure?
- **Substitute products and services:** are there alternatives to what you do that retailers or customers might use?
- **Power of suppliers:** if there are relatively few suppliers, they can make rules and deals that impact on your profitability.
- **Current competitors:** rivalry among current competitors impacts on the attractiveness of a given market. How competitive is this market?

 To hear Michael Porter outline his thinking on competition, check out this video:

https://www.youtube.com/watch?v=mYF2_FBCvXw

How to use the Five Forces Model

The Five Forces Model does not produce an answer – it still requires interpretation. So, the easiest way to start is by asking yourself several key questions under each competitive force. It might also help if you try to keep in mind this diagram. This shows the forces are connected and in a dynamic relationship.

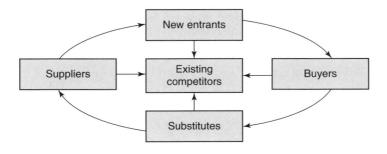

Case study

Children Creche Co. (CCC)

CCC is a small company providing childcare services directly to parents through a network of neighbourhood nurseries. It has heard that a large local business will be considering whether to continue using its current supplier Happy Kids Co. (HKC) to provide childcare onsite for employees. This contract could be worth £1.5 m over three years. The CEO and senior team of CCC are trying to decide what to do. This would be a big contract for them.

The model encourages the CEO and their team to ask some key questions under each force:

1. **New entrants:** is it easy to enter the market or are there economic or legal barriers to entry?

   - *Does it cost a lot to set up in competition?* So, for example, it is expensive to start a railway and you need a licence. For CCC, taking over an existing facility at the workplace probably would not be expensive. And it has licences already.

   - *Is it difficult to persuade consumers/users to switch from existing providers?* Persuading people to switch from PCs to Macs is a challenge. But, even if parents like HKC – the existing supplier – the fact the company is paying CCC presumably makes it less of a challenge.

   - *Do existing providers have a scale-independent cost advantage?* This is a unique advantage, such as a patent. In the case of CCC, if it or its rivals have a unique accredited training programme for childcare workers, then this could be a similar advantage.

2. **Buyer's power:**
   - *Is scale or volume important in this transaction?* Walmart can buy in bulk more cheaply than a local store and so has a massive advantage. HKC – the current provider – may offer a very good deal if it is already working for many companies.
   - *How is the cost of supplying the service made up?* If a large part of the cost is profit, then a buyer who knows this will bargain hard. Presumably, for CCC, labour is the big cost. So, it needs to look at salaries carefully.
   - *Is there the potential for the buyer to become a provider?* Technically, this is known as backwards integration. So, a mobile phone manufacturer might set up its own phone network. CCC might ask if the company could set up its own childcare provision and not use an external supplier.

3. **Substitute products and services:** is it easy to find an alternative?
   - *How readily available and cost comparable are substitutes?* In the mobile phone industry, the big providers are all similar and the costs of switching very small – hence long contracts. For our childcare agency, this might be a challenge if, for example, the company was considering giving employees childcare vouchers too, allowing them to buy privately.

4. **Power of suppliers:** suppliers are an important part of the framework, too.
   - *What is the ratio of buyers to sellers?* Sellers have lots of say on the cost and form of supply, if there are few of them relative to buyers, e.g. directory enquiries before deregulation was a monopoly, now it is a free market. Or, if suppliers do not need to use you as a channel, then this can create problems: Apple deciding to sell direct to customers caused challenges for computer resellers. CCC should consider whether many other organisations are in competition for this contract. If not, it has a better position.

5. **Current competitors:** is there significant rivalry in competitors?

- *How much competition is there?* For our childcare agency, it again might want to consider how many competitors there are apart from the incumbent.
- *Is it difficult to compare competitors?* It is more difficult if competitors are very different. For example, you could agree that trains compete with buses in terms of getting from A to B. But they are very different in terms of who uses them and why. Would the childcare vouchers compete for CCC business?
- *Are there any very high exit barriers?* In other words, is it difficult – economically, emotionally or legally – to leave the market? For example, redundancy costs may be high. So, for CCC, closing down the crèche in the future could cause a big reputational challenge.

Call to action

- Can you identify your key competitors?
- Can you identify where they compete and how important this is to you?
- Are you able to distinguish your competitive advantage?
- What are the key competitive forces you need to consider in terms of entering a market that seems attractive? Are there any markets you should exit?

Step **7**

Focus your energy: making the right choices

After reading this step you will be able to:

- Understand the key issues in deciding new strategic direction
- Identify the four key choices in strategy direction
- Understand the 6Cs needed when making a strategic choice
- Identify the best strategic option.

The reality is that you can never have enough resources, enough capital or enough time to do everything. So, the secret of success is to focus and direct attention on a specific approach, putting in enough energy and resources to deliver a specific outcome.

Deciding this strategic direction, however, can be a major challenge. Igor Ansoff, US strategy guru, developed a matrix that helps focus your attention. Helpfully, he argues that you have only four main strategic options – or four key choices – when planning new directions. So, the good news is you simply need to choose one or more of these.

Having said that each of these options has varying levels of:

- **risk:** what might go wrong
- **difficulty:** how hard it is to do.

We will explore the implications of this in the 6Cs.

How to decide where to focus

Ansoff says there are two key choice dimensions you need to be concerned about:

- **Markets:** the people who buy or use your company's products or services – called customers, consumers or service users.
- **Products:** the things you make or sell – these can be products, services or offerings.

Each of these dimensions has a binary aspect – that is, they are either existing or new.

In the case of markets, this means a customer can either be an existing customer or a new (potential) one.

Equally, a product can be an existing one or a new (yet to be produced or marketed) one.

By putting these elements together, we have another useful 2×2 strategic matrix.

Offerings/Services/Products

	Existing	New
Existing (Customers/Consumers/Users)	1.	2.
New (Customers/Consumers/Users)	3.	4.

This matrix then gives you four strategic choices or, more properly, emphases, since you may well do a number of these together but to different degrees.

These choices are:

- **Box 1: existing offerings for existing customers.** Persuading current customers to buy more of your existing products or services. So, if you ran a fruit shop, you could try to persuade the people who normally come into the shop to buy an apple to buy more. (Offer six for the price of five?) If you were an online retailer like Amazon, you might try to persuade book buyers to buy more, by saying 'three for the price of two offer on books'.

- **Box 2: new offerings for existing customers.** Developing new products or services for existing customers. So, back in the fruit shop, you could try to persuade customers to buy bread as well as fruit or maybe offer to deliver vegetable boxes. Or Amazon could try to persuade you to use them for streaming films and not just buying books. (Sound familiar?)

- **Box 3: new customers for existing offerings.** Persuading new customers to adopt current offerings – for example, in your fruit shop, you might try to persuade schools to bulk buy fruit for children at lunchtime. Amazon might decide to open an operation in a new country or even to set up a special website offering the same products in different languages.

- **Box 4: new offerings for new customers.** This is the radical innovation option when you try to persuade brand new people to adopt brand new offerings. As a fruit seller, you could decide to start selling smoothies to local health clubs. And Amazon could decide to offer cloud storage for companies that want secure 24/7 data storage.

What does it take to be good in each box?

So, you can argue that you want to do all four. But Ansoff cautions here. And our experience suggests that he is right. Each box is different and you need to be careful where you operate. So, the boxes:

- are not all equally easy to operate in
- require different competencies from you as a business
- have degrees of risk associated with them.

Think about what it takes to be successful in each box. Make some notes below.

What competencies/skills/knowledge do you need to work effectively in each box? Which are the riskiest and which are the safest?	
1.	2.
3.	4.

The 6Cs checklist of choice

When thinking about how successful you might be in any one quadrant, you should consider a variant on the 6Cs checklist we used in the book's introduction.

- **Context:** what does your environmental scan – PEST and SWOT – tell you about the opportunity? Before taking action, you need to explore the market in which you want to work – the global fast food market, the UK banana market, London's tourist market, etc. And there are some further questions arising from that first one. For example, are there enough wealthy potential customers with enough capacity to deliver your sales target for high-end jewellery? Does the channel you want to use – off-the-page advertising or online – work in that setting? Does your brand have enough traction to generate new business now – or do you need to raise awareness before you can do sales? Deciding honestly and objectively on your context will help in your plan.

- **Competencies:** do you have the skills, knowledge and abilities to make any strategic change in your approach? So, again, there are some further detailed questions. What experience do you have, or need, to work in the new option you have in mind? Do you know what the best channel or channel mix is for the new strategy? Do you have, or can you get, the skills you need to underpin the change? Launching into an initiative without competencies will end in tears or burnout.

- **Competition:** who else is in the space you would like to occupy or explore – and how strong are they? There are some further questions here, too. Which competitors are doing the same thing? Are any competitors more effective in the channel you want to use – and, if so, how could you gain a competitive edge? Look at how Apple's iPad distinguished itself very successfully from other tablets. Are there other channels available for you to use that would help deal with competition?

- **Cash:** do you have enough capital to invest in the new strategic area? This is a tough question. Have you costed all aspects of the initiative – from funding new manufacturing capacity to hiring staff? Do you have the £1 m or more you need for the big TV campaign – and how long can you spend that amount to get a result? Is another, larger company able to outspend you and so maintain its dominance in the market? You need a properly costed plan and then to be prepared to invest for long enough.

- **Commitment:** this is really the killer question. Does your senior team or board appreciate the time and effort they need to give for any initiative? Do they, and maybe even you, appreciate the risks – financial and reputational – associated with the option you have chosen? Are those key stakeholders happy to stake out a claim for an area of activity and re-orientate policy or service to ensure you deliver? If you have not got commitment, all the rest will not work.

- **Companions:** you need to decide who you need to have on board in order to succeed in your chosen focus. These companions – stakeholders – could range all the way from senior managers to suppliers to staff colleagues. They can help you succeed in one or more of the quadrants. It is worth listing whose help, support or even sanction you need in a specific quadrant.

Stick to your knitting: why work outside box 1?

Ansoff suggests you always look to operate in box 1 first. This is sensible. After all, it consists of the people and the products you know. Tom Peters, management guru, famously talked about 'sticking to your knitting' as a way of focusing attention on current business with current customers.

The reality is that, in many organisations, individuals are desperate to work outside box 1. What is the lure? There are a number of reasons people want to move out of box 1, in our experience, including:

- **boredom:** being effective in box 1 can be quite boring, as it involves simply doing existing things well; those things include practical issues, like keeping the database up to date or ensuring that customer service is high quality

- **excitement:** working outside box 1, especially in box 4, can seem quite fun and exciting – it is the innovators and entrepreneurs box – so, by working here, you can feel like someone who is really pushing at the boundaries.

Just to be clear, working outside box 1 is probably something you should do, but it is essential not to neglect box 1, since that is where your core is.

There is a generally accepted order in which to think about the four strategy options. You should first consider whether you could, for example, gain more market share with your current offerings in your current markets (market penetration strategy). Next, consider whether you can develop new offerings of potential interest to your current markets (offering development strategy). Then, consider whether you can find or develop new markets for your current offerings (market development strategy). Finally, review opportunities to develop new offerings for new markets (diversification strategy). This sequence is based on degree of difficulty.

 **Exercise**

Take a minute to think about advising the senior marketing team at CardCo. It runs a chain of greetings card shops and is keen to expand. So it considers each of the four options. What options might you come up with quickly to help the company focus its attention in each of the four boxes? See our answer in the following case study.

	Existing offerings	**New offerings**
Existing markets	1. Market penetration strategy	2. Offering development strategy
New markets	3. Market development strategy	4. Diversification strategy

Case study

Strategy options for CardCo: our answer

So, how did you do in our case study? Here is our take on what they might do in each of the four boxes. Compare it to your answer.

Market penetration strategy

CardCo could start by encouraging its current customers to use its shops more frequently. Having previously sold mostly birthday cards, CardCo could start promoting cards for many different occasions – divorce, house moving, Bar and Bat Mitzvahs, etc. (This is, essentially, the same offering.)

Alternatively, CardCo could try to attract customers of other card shops to switch to it. This would make sense if CardCo noticed a lot of weaknesses in its competitors. If Clinton Cards seems a little boring, CardCo could try to lure its customers in, perhaps with discounts.

Offering development strategy

Next, CardCo management should consider some new offering development possibilities.

Since it sells cards in its shops, it could develop gifts to accompany the cards: flowers, mugs or chocolates. It could open a coffee shop for browsers. It could sell e-readers.

Market development strategy

CardCo should also look for new markets whose needs might be met by its current offerings.

CardCo might try to identify new potential customers. If it had been encouraging use only by consumers, it might go after businesses with corporate cards. ('Motivate your staff or customers by sending them a card!')

Second, CardCo might seek additional distribution channels. If it has been selling only through its own shops, it might add other channels (e.g. having a counter in a department store or selling cards online.)

Finally, CardCo might consider selling in new geographic locations. If the company sold only in the North East of the UK, it could consider adding the North West, London or, even, opening markets in Europe.

Diversification strategy

This is the most challenging and risky of the four boxes, but also the box in which really creative ideas happen. CardCo could decide to sell stationery supplies to businesses or open a wholefood café in-store to attract passersby.

In this context, it is worth thinking about how Waterstones has tried, as part of its business recovery strategy, to operate in all four boxes.

 To check out Clare Segal and Bernard Ross sharing more on the practical application of focusing on different boxes, have a look at:

www.thebusinessgym.net

 Exercise

Use the matrix below in one of two ways:

- Outline how you might develop the business or team in which you work in each box. Where should you focus to improve profitability? What new things could you do and with whom? If you were in charge, how would you develop each box? Think about money as a resource – if you had £100 k to invest, where would you invest it? What is your rationale for that choice?

- Think about yourself in terms of your career matrix. What should you do to improve your current profile or contribution in

Products/Services/Offerings

	Existing	*New*
Existing	1.	2.
New	3.	4.

Customers/Consumers/Users

your current team (box 1)? And in what way should you develop your skills/new products (box 2)? Who else could you offer to help (new internal customers) to advance (box 3)? Should you think about a whole new job with a new skill set (box 4)? Where should you focus to improve your chances of promotion? Think about time as a resource – if you had eight hours to invest, where would you invest it?

Remember to use the 6Cs to be clear on where to focus your energy. Where might you be most effective?

Call to action

- Can you map out what are the key opportunities that you, your team or organisation have – and what the risks and consequences are for each?

- Are you clear where you should focus your strategic attention – for your organisation, department or team? (Or even for yourself.)

- If you want to move outside box 1, are you clear why you should do this? Where should your next move be?

- Are you clear how you might change your strategy over time? Do you need to keep working in box 2 or 3?

- Next time you are at a meeting talking through options, see if you can fit the choices being discussed into one or more of the boxes. Then mention the 6Cs as a way to assess practicality.

Step 8

Think outside the box: using innovation to develop new ideas

After reading this step you will be able to:

- Know how to organise an innovation session to help inform strategy
- Understand how to think up some radically different ideas
- Understand how to engage people in your innovation session
- Select a genuinely useful idea.

Think the unthinkable

Sometimes, you are trying to generate a new approach as part of your strategy – because your existing approach seems to be running out of steam, you are faced with a crisis or maybe just because you are in a business where you have to keep coming up with new ideas. Again, as a junior manager, this may be an area where you actually have an advantage – bringing the fresh thinking that is so often valued.

You may, of course, be the kind of lonely business genius who comes up with ideas alone. But, if you are not, then you may want to try to manage the process of generating ideas by organising a creativity and innovation session – sometimes called a brainstorm.

This step offers you a simple and straightforward framework to develop a new idea that can feed into your strategy. Importantly, the framework is one that you can use with colleagues.

How to be systematically creative

 In business you cannot wait for sudden inspiration. So, you need to be able to turn on inspiration like a tap when you need it.

Brainstorming seems to have a bad reputation as a great way to waste time and a lot of flipcharts and sticky notes. A good brainstorm involves disciplined, but creative, thinking for a short period of time with the aim of coming up with some very specific possibilities to change or develop strategy.

Here is a simple step-by-step guide to running your first successful strategic brainstorm.

1: Decide the challenge or issue you want to tackle

You need to focus on a very specific issue that might be solvable. Choose a topic like 'how to reach the under 16s market', 'how to reduce costs by 10 per cent' or 'how to secure PR for the company for free'. Any of these topics, or a topic of similar granularity, will produce a focused outcome. (Remember, though, the key issue with creativity is you have to be prepared to accept that ideas generated might not work out. So, the outcome is not guaranteed to be a *good* idea.)

2: Decide the people you want to have in the room

There are some people who are good at being creative and innovative and some people who are not. So try to get as many of the former in the room to start with. (And keep some of those cynics for later . . . they *will* have a use.) In general, a small group is easier to manage than a big group – there seems to be a magic number of around about 8 or 10. The idea is to keep your group small enough to stay focused but not so small that there is no diversity of opinion.

3: Sort out the logistics and the structure

- **Do find a place different from where people normally work.** It does not need to be off-site – though that helps – but even meeting in a different part of the building or in a room without a table can make a big difference. Also, think about having an independent facilitator. A skilled facilitator will help manage the group without fear or favour and will bring out people who are quiet and calm rather than those who are noisy.

- **Do not try to have an all-day brainstorm** – your brain and everyone else's will turn to mush. We suggest an ideal time is 1.5 hours – long enough to get the juices flowing but not so long that it turns into a slog. Flipcharts and sticky notes are always useful to capture ideas. Make it clear in your invitation to the other brainstormers that you are looking for a burst of mental energy.

4: Generate ideas

Before you begin the session, it is worth rolling out some broad ground rules so people understand that you are talking about creativity, but within rules.

State the purpose of the session or the desired outcome as a question – for example, 'How can we reach the under 16s market?'

If appropriate, invite restatements of this question from participants. So, these might include: 'How to persuade the under 16s market to come to us?' 'How to appeal to girls under 16?' Notice the topic is always framed as a question. Decide on one of these restatements to use as the focus – you can always come back to the others later. Write this down at the top of a flipchart.

On another flipchart, put down what you currently know or believe to be the current case about this question. So, this should include any data you have about the current demographics of your customers or about why people like or dislike your offering. When you have captured this, put it off to one side so that people can refer to it as necessary.

If appropriate, on a third flipchart, consider an organisation, a product or a service that you believe is successful in reaching the under 16s market. Try to analyse why they might be successful. Is it their brand, the price point, the channel they use, or what? Keep this in mind and in sight, too. So, with the three flipcharts prepared you are ready to start brainstorming.

Now, try for what we call a burst – a burst is an intensive period of, perhaps, 10 minutes when people can shout out ideas on how to answer the question written on the flipchart. Or, as an alternative, participants can write ideas on sticky notes and put them on a wall. We generally favour the sticky notes approach, since that allows you to move and cluster the ideas easily.

5: Cluster and compare

Now cluster your ideas. See if any can be sensibly combined. And then rate them. Again, we prefer the simple ABC method.

Make some ideas As – useful. Bs are less useful. And Cs too weird or weak to be worth looking at just now.

If you have a group of 8–10 people, it is, possibly, worthwhile asking smaller groups of 3 or 4 to choose one of these ideas to work up and bring back to the group. This might then lead to a further whittling down of ideas to end up with two or three that need a full business case.

Before you finish, it is always worth going back to one of the C ideas that was dismissed right at the start of the session. There could be the gem of a real possibility in this idea so it is worth a quick check. Get everyone to brainstorm 'how could we make this idea work?' as this question often promotes some lateral thinking. (See **Challenge 4** on pivoting and how Twitter was developed.)

6: Work up and improve

Now you need to work on the ideas and try to decide which of them genuinely are useful or might have some traction. There are lots of different ways to do this and one of the most useful is called Six Thinking Hats. Let us look at how to use this technique.

Six Thinking Hats: how to work out what is a good idea

Six Thinking Hats (6TH) was developed by internationally respected brain consultant Edward de Bono. His work is now widely used in education and business. If people in your team or organisation are not used to this technique, it would be great for you to introduce it.

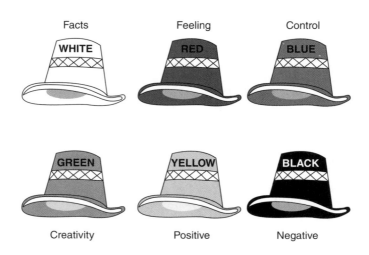

| Facts | Feeling | Control |
| WHITE | RED | BLUE |

| GREEN | YELLOW | BLACK |
| Creativity | Positive | Negative |

6TH is a useful technique for helping groups:

- engage in developing and sharing ideas as a group
- make better decisions about which ideas to progress
- align their thinking using parallel rather than conflicted thinking.

The technique is based on the idea that there are six imaginary thinking hats. Each hat is a different colour and represents a different type of thinking. When you put on a hat, you operate exclusively in that mode of thinking. When you change from one hat to another, you change thinking modes. And, importantly, everyone thinks the same way at the same time, so avoiding futile 'Tis' 'Tisn't' conflict.

de Bono uses a hats metaphor because:

- there is a link between thinking and hats – for example, 'put on your thinking cap' – so, the idea makes sense to people when you explain it to them
- hats can be put on or off very easily; this encourages people to switch and think in different ways rather than to stay stuck in one.

Let us consider the hats and how they encourage structured thinking sequences to help decide if an idea is a useful strategic contribution or a fun but, ultimately, purposeless diversion.

The white hat

Think of printed reports, books or even newspapers. The paper is usually white. The white hat, like paper, is concerned with data and information – facts, not opinion.

There are specific questions associated with this hat:

- What information do we have or do we need?
- What information would we like to have and how would we get it?

When wearing the white hat, you focus on facts and information, for example:

- 'Let's stop the argument and have some white-hat thinking. What do we know about the new legislation and how it will impact on our work?'
- 'We badly need some white-hat thinking here. What do we know about the needs and interests of under 16s?'

The red hat

For the red hat, you should think of fire. The focus here is on feelings and intuition. When using the red hat, you are allowed to put forward ideas and opinions that are not underpinned by logic or data. In fact, in red-hat mode, you are not obliged to, nor should people ask you to, explain or justify your responses. There are dangers, of course, when prejudices can take over. But gut feel can be important and, like the other hats, the red hat can be used only at an agreed time in the discussion.

- 'From a red-hat point of view, I have to say that idea sounds like a fantasy that just won't deliver any practical payoff.'
- 'Well, we've talked about the two options. Can we just go around the room now and hear which of the ideas is most exciting to everyone?'

The black hat

For this hat, de Bono encourages you to think of a judge's robes. The job of the judge is to critically examine all the evidence and dismiss anything that is not relevant or purposeful. So, the black hat is the caution hat, designed to let you point out challenges, drawbacks, difficulties and problems in any proposed idea.

The black hat is the most widely used hat in business. It is useful – since it stops thinking that is unrealistic. But, because critical thinking is sometimes overvalued, it is quite easy to overuse it. Indeed, some people never seem to take it off. This is why it is important to have a range of hats.

In black-hat mode, you may find yourself saying:

- 'Hang on. We need some black-hat thinking now, before we get carried away. What are the difficulties? What are the dangers? What could go wrong with this approach?'

The yellow hat

This hat takes its colour from sunshine – and builds an association with positivity. The yellow hat represents logical positive thinking. Use this hat to establish payoffs, benefits and potential. You can also use it specifically for feasibility – can we make this approach or idea work?

The yellow hat complements the black hat – it allows you to look at the same issue or idea just from a different perspective. The logical as well as positive nature of the yellow hat is key. Yellow-hat contributions must be optimistic *and* realistic.

Many individuals and groups find this kind of thinking less natural than the black-hat critical approach. It takes more conscious effort sometimes to find value and benefits, especially if the idea is quite radical. Wearing the yellow hat you might find yourself saying:

- 'OK, we've had all the downsides, thanks to the black hat. Let's change gear and wear the yellow hat. What benefit or potential is there in this suggestion?'
- 'Jan, you offered really useful critical ideas earlier. Let me push you to come up with positive responses here. What might be the benefits to a significant price reduction?'

The green hat

The green hat is designed to encourage you to think of nature, growing plants, photosynthesis – the change from one energy to another. So, this hat is the creative alternative hat. In green hat you are encouraged to think of different ways to reframe the project.

The focus here is on variations to existing ideas. It is for possibilities, even if they are remote. Like the red hat, the green hat does not need to have a logical base. This is a time for suggestions, for ideas, for possibilities. In a way, your initial brainstorm was really a green-hat approach.

You cannot force participants to have creative ideas. But it is reasonable to ask them to apply some imaginative thinking. In this situation, you might find yourself saying:

- 'It looks like none of the ideas we have is usable in the current form. Let's choose a couple and try some green-hat thinking to see how they might be adapted to work.'
- 'Well, we've agreed that we need to focus on this idea. Let's just see if we can come up with some variations that might give us a lot more flexibility.'

The blue hat

The emphasis here, de Bono suggests, is on cool, blue sky and overview. This hat is most useful for controlling or managing the thinking process. Unlike all the others, only one person wears the blue hat, in the role of facilitator or chair.

If you are wearing the blue hat, you are responsible for structuring the thinking of the group. This can mean several things. One obvious one is that you plan the sequence of the hats – see below. Or it can be that you call people to account for the kind of thinking they are sharing – 'George I need you to get back into yellow hat. You are sounding a bit black hat-ish.' Or you may take responsibility for changing the thinking sequence by saying, 'We seem a bit stuck here, shall we try a couple of minutes of green hat to see if we can reframe the idea and come up with a new one?'

Finally, the blue hat asks for, or offers, summaries. It can also draw out conclusions. Wearing blue hat, you might, typically, say:

- 'Wearing my blue hat, I think we've spent the last 20 minutes looking for someone to blame for this mess. But we have not made any constructive suggestions at all. So I'm going to suggest we move to green hat to come up with some new ideas.'

 For an animated PowerPoint explaining Six Thinking Hats, have a look at:

https://www.youtube.com/watch?v=SzlLDLnqJ98

Sequencing thinking . . . and hats

A key skill in using 6TH is that of sequencing. This is choosing the right order of thinking to explore an issue. An agreed sequence stops people getting stuck in any one hat or a couple of participants dominating proceedings as they bounce back and forth between yellow and black.

The table below is a typical sequence for a meeting to discuss an idea.

Hat	Purpose	Time
Blue	Lays out the proposed sequence of hats. Explains the proposition or idea that is going to be discussed.	2 mins
White	Gives any facts or data behind the idea – e.g. customer data, who else has tried it, etc.	2 mins
Red	Initial feelings or intuitions on the idea from around the group. It is important that everyone is encouraged to share their ideas.	2 mins
Yellow	How the idea could be made to work and its advantages.	3 mins
Black	Why the idea might not work. Any negative consequences.	2 mins
Green	Building on the original idea to produce something stronger or improved.	3 mins
Red	Everyone's feelings about the idea as it is now. What does their gut or intuition tell them?	2 mins
Black	Issues to be careful of in making any decision. A reality check.	2 mins
Red	Feelings about whether or not to go ahead. A final check around the group making sure people are aligned. (Or not.)	2 mins
White/Blue	Conclusions summarised and next steps agreed.	2 mins

Things to note:

- **Not categories:** the six hats are not descriptions or categories of thinkers. Every person in the group should be able to use every hat. It is likely that people will have a preference for one hat over another, but they must be able to use all of them.

- **Fast and focused:** 6TH works best when the thinking is fast and focused. So, in the example above, you can see that only

2–3 minutes are devoted to each hat. This ensures that people do not start to wander in their thinking. Or get stuck.

- **Individual or group:** you do not need to use 6TH only in groups, you can also use it by yourself to structure and organise your own thinking. This is helpful if you are:

  - organising a report: use blue hat as a structure for the report and for executive summaries; use yellow and black hat for advantages and disadvantages of any action recommended or for further analysis

  - thinking through a challenge with a colleague: talk to them using the hats approach – you do not have to be overt about it; 'OK, there's a problem. How serious do you feel it is?' (red). 'What exactly do you know about the impact?' (white). 'So, what should you do?' (green). And so on . . .

 To see a video on Six Thinking Hats in use during a meeting, visit:

www.thebusinessgym.net

Case study

Motorola develops a new product

Despite some difficult times, Motorola is a global leader in communications. In 2002, the company wanted to create a high-end communications product.

They held a 6TH innovation meeting for managers to develop a new high-tech, hand-held device for people who wanted the latest technology.

The first day was a white-hat process. Profiles were constructed for existing and target consumers: age, income, education and habits. This gave managers a detailed picture of their possible market and their needs.

On day two, the facilitator led the group through a green-hat session to generate ideas for the 'product for the future' against these profiles. Then, each idea was assessed using yellow- and black-hat thinking. This was followed by the group using red-hat thinking to prioritise what they felt were the best ideas.

The group then used white-hat data from the profiles to discuss a 'Day in the life' of a consumer, e.g. how they might use the product from waking up to bedtime. Should it have an alarm? Or be able to play music files? The group dissected the day hour by hour to ensure that the product was ideal for the target market. Green hat was also used to consider wider uses.

The result was a device called the Accompli.

 Exercise

Let us assume you know for sure that in three years' time the products or services you currently provide will be of little or no value. So, you have a maximum of three years to come up with a radical new business idea. You would like to keep the current staff and hold on to your customers, but you will be unable to make whatever you currently make, or deliver whatever service you currently deliver.

Grab a flipchart. Take five minutes to come up with as many new business ideas that you can think of that you could supply to current customers with the current workforce skillset (green hat).

Now ABC those ideas in red hat:

- As = the ones that most appeal to you
- Bs = the ones that slightly appeal
- Cs = the ones that appeal least.

Put aside the Bs and Cs. Looking at each A one by one, start by using the white hat. What do you know about the costs associated with this option, its acceptability to your customer base and the core competencies you have?

Next, take each of your As and:

- put on the yellow hat for 60 seconds – now you have some facts about it, what real advantages or positives does this idea have?

- put on the black hat for 60 seconds – what negatives or pitfalls does this idea have?
- put on the red hat for 30 seconds – do you feel any of the ideas stand out? Are any of them worth progressing to the next level of detail?

If the answer is yes, go back to white hat and plan how you might take it forward and who will do this.

If the answer is no, then try green hat to see if you can come up with an improved idea – and then go back to the start of the loop again.

Call to action

- Can you describe the key stages in a brainstorm – what are they?
- What do you need to be careful about in a brainstorm?
- On what topic might you practise brainstorming?
- What kind of thinking does each of the hats offer?
- When else might you use 6TH apart from meetings and brainstorms?

Step 9

Explore the territory: building a strategy map

After reading this step you will be able to:

- Explain your strategy simply using a leading strategy tool
- Understand how to tie your strategic ideas together in a one-page diagram
- Appreciate the key perspectives in a BSC/ strategy map
- Identify the how/why logic in a strategy.

To gain attention in the crowded business mindspace, you need to find a way to express any strategy simply and understandably – but the expression also needs to reflect the complexity of relationships and activities in your business, department or team. That is a tall order. And there are not many ways to do that.

More than that, if you are looking for a unified way to pull together the various tools in the book, then the Kaplan and Norton strategy map and balanced scorecard is probably your best opportunity.

We have included this framework partly because, if you work for any kind of big company, probably you will come up against it at some point. See the box below for some statistics on uptake in larger businesses.

At its simplest, the strategy map describes how an organisation will deliver its strategy expressed as a one-page systems diagram. Note, though, that the one page is part of a linked series of three elements.

The strategy map outlines the fundamental business logic of the plan, demonstrates the implications for internal and external stakeholders, codifies the organisational competencies needed, explores what kind of skills and knowledge staff need, and identifies what resources need to be invested. This is what we are going to focus on here.

This is, generally, complemented by a balanced scorecard (BSC) to track how effectively the plan is being delivered and an implementation plan to show how the activities to deliver the plan will be sequenced and rolled out. We are not going to explore these here – but there is more about them in the video mentioned below.

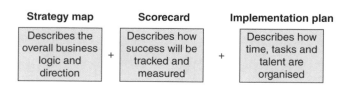

The wisdom of crowds

Part of the attraction of using the BSC is that the approach has significant traction. Many companies, including 70 per cent of Fortune 500 companies and 60 per cent of the FTSE 100 companies, use it. So, if you adopt the model, you can gain access to an enormous number of examples with which to compare your own company's or team's practice. (The strategy map can be used at almost any level of an organisation.)

We have also used the strategy map model with a number of public sector and charity organisations.

The IFRC, the largest humanitarian organisation in the world, is using a strategy map we helped develop over 18 months to grow from a US$30 bn organisation to US$50 bn working across almost 200 nations.

At the other end of the size and geography spectrum, we worked with the leadership team at Shepway District Council to create a map of how to make the council work in a more joined-up way.

Major companies using the BSC model include Ford Motor Company, Tesco, BT, DuPont, Hilton Hotels, IBM, etc.

What is the balanced scorecard (BSC)?

Two US academics, Robert Kaplan and David Norton, developed the BSC methodology during the 1990s. The methodology has since moved through a number of iterations. Originally, the balanced scorecard simply asked you to measure the critical success factors in running a successful organisation. It focused, as the name suggests, on two simple dimensions:

- **balancing the key perspectives in an organisation:** customers, internal processes, learning and growth, and finance (these are seen as interdependent)
- **scoring and tracking a small number of metrics and measures:** critical success factors that drive success in each of these perspectives.

Since this first incarnation, Kaplan and Norton's thinking has moved on and the perspectives are now organised in a sequence – hence the map concept.

 To get some background on the theory of BSC, watch this animation at:

http://balancedscorecard.org/training/BSC_Overview_Private/player.html

How to build a strategy map

You need to think of your strategy as being composed of a number of perspectives or key areas. The four classic perspectives are finance, customer, capacities and learning and growth. These perspectives combine in sequence to make your map.

The sequence in which you organise the perspectives is important.

 Good financial results come about from meeting customer needs. And you meet those by having effective internal processes.

To deliver these processes, you need people who are learning and growing. Organising the perspectives properly ensures that the strategy combines both external outcomes (financial success, customer satisfaction) and internal inputs (what capacities are needed to achieve the outcomes and what skills are needed from people).

Below is a diagram showing what is called the how/why logic of a map. This is important, since strategy is, essentially, a series of hypotheses – demonstrating what impacts on what.

'Strategy implies the movement of an organisation from its present position to a desirable but uncertain future position. Because the organisation has never been to this future position, its intended pathway involves a series of linked hypotheses.'

Kaplan and Norton

How/why logic

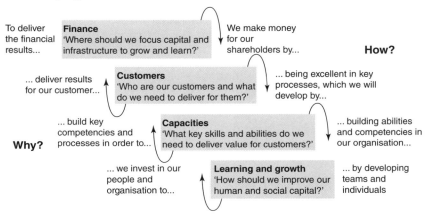

Within each perspective are a number of objectives – specific high-level statements of outcome. (Kaplan and Norton use the word objectives to mean high-level statement of outcome rather than the classic SMART objectives – specific, measurable, agreed, realistic and time-bound.) For this reason, the objectives need to be connected to each other in a cause-and-effect logic – creating a linked narrative. See the diagram illustrating this after the case study.

Case study

South West Airlines

The strategy map that follows this case study is based on one of the earliest developed, for South West Airlines (SWA) in the USA. SWA essentially invented the low-cost business model now used worldwide by many airlines. (One indicator of the power of their map, and this approach generally, is that it has been borrowed so often by other airlines.)

SWA began with some drivers about the need to use their expensive planes more effectively and to offer lower fares to encourage passengers to fly with them rather than competitors. They also needed to persuade staff to work more flexibly and to be committed to helping turn the planes around fast to help ensure more in-the-air time.

Notice down the left-hand side of the diagram below the four perspectives of a BSC at work, showing a hierarchical logic. So, to make money – finance – you need to satisfy customer needs. These needs are met by having strong internal processes (capacities). And to achieve the process improvements requires a learning and growth strategy that engages and develops staff and builds an appropriate culture.

The objectives – the bubbles on the right-hand side – show what activity must take place in each perspective to deliver the overall goal of running a profitable airline. The objectives also follow a vertical logic – with the down path answering the question 'how?' and the up path answering 'why?'

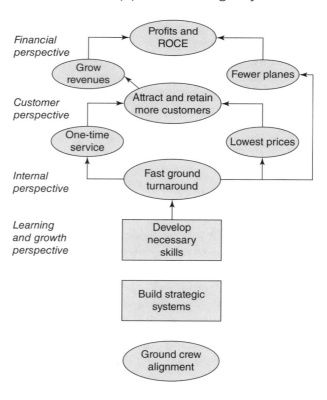

This simple model contains profound insights into how to run a successful low-cost airline. Its simplicity is a key feature of an effective strategy map.

You normally begin with the *how* logic when creating a map, reading it from the top perspective to the bottom:

How will we succeed in our strategy?	By meeting our financial objectives.
How will we meet the financial objectives?	By delivering value to our customers and shareholders.
How will we be sure to deliver to our customers and shareholders?	By excelling in key internal business processes – capacities.
How can we be sure we are excellent in those processes?	By learning and improving as individuals and teams.

If you read the map from the bottom perspective to the top, it should explain *why* you have chosen the objectives in each perspective, as shown below:

Why are we learning and growing in this way?	In order to excel in our internal processes – capacities.
Why are we focusing on those particular processes?	To deliver a high-quality service to our customers.
Why do we need to deliver this service to our customers and shareholders?	To ensure we achieve our financial objectives.
Why do we need to achieve the financial objectives?	To succeed in our strategy and move towards our vision.

 Create a strategy map for an events venue

Have a go at making a map by developing one for a party venue setting in London. We have given you their *vision* and *mission*. And they have three big-ticket goals or overarching results they want to achieve. Can you work out what the how/why logic should be?

There is no right answer. And you do not need to have the 11 objectives in the boxes. See what you can do.

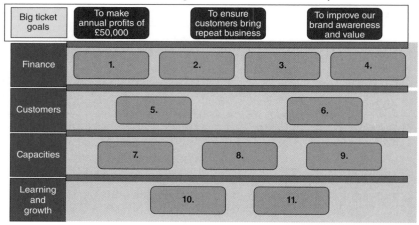

Our vision: **To be the first choice 'special occasions' and party venue in London**
Our mission: **To offer outstanding customer service at affordable prices**

Big ticket goals	To make annual profits of £50,000	To ensure customers bring repeat business	To improve our brand awareness and value
Finance	1.	2.	3. 4.
Customers	5.		6.
Capacities	7.	8.	9.
Learning and growth	10.	11.	

To see a practical example of a strategy map building up, watch this animation at:

www.thebusinessgym.net

And, if you visit, we will show you our answer to the venue map problem.

  Create your own strategy map

The easiest way to create a strategy map is with those three trusted tools:

- a flipchart
- some felt markers
- a pack of sticky notes.

Use the flipchart as the scorecard frame. Turn it on its side and mark it up like the framework above, showing the perspectives. Use the pen and sticky notes to capture draft objectives. (You can convert this rough and ready approach to a beautiful, elegant PowerPoint later.)

Begin by setting some long-term, big ticket goals like those above. These might relate to:

- a specific profit goal you have
- a customer acquisition or retention goal
- a new product development goal
- a market growth goal.

You then need to reflect on how the logic will work through the perspectives to meet these goals. Consider the questions in the how/why diagram (above) relevant to each perspective. The answers to the questions are your objectives.

Once you have agreed the objectives in the top perspective, move to the next one, asking the key questions for that one. Make sure you follow the how/why logic. The objectives in one perspective should explain how you plan to achieve the objectives in the perspective above.

Continue down the map until you have objectives populating each of the perspectives. If it seems, on reflection, that an objective would be better suited in another perspective, do not be afraid to move it. You can always move it back. And, likewise, do not be afraid to put down lots of objectives initially, as you can combine them later.

When identifying objectives, it is important to consider whether they:

- **remain true to your VMVC from Step 2:** the map is designed to *translate* your strategy, so it should not contradict the fundamental way you want to work; it should, rather, be a natural expression of your VMVC
- **capture the key things you need to be successful:** remember, the map does not describe everything so, what are the few – 10–15 – objectives that are *critical* to your success?
- **flow from your overarching strategic aims:** the objectives describe how you will achieve what you need to do; the aims – at the top of the map – represent the major results you want to achieve; all objectives should lead to or from these.

After your first draft, review the quality of the map and think about three questions:

- **How many objectives are there?** Focus is important. If you have more than 15 overall, you risk an overload of data when measuring progress on the scorecard. Many BSC projects collapse because of the data burden. Capping the number of objectives ensures focus and simplicity.
- **What is the granularity of the objectives?** Are they too general (e.g. develop staff), too specific (e.g. improve creativity skills among tier three middle managers) or properly balanced (e.g. develop a more entrepreneurial culture among all staff)?
- **Does the map communicate the key internal and external priorities?** Does it tell the story of your strategy in an understandable way that stakeholders can identify with? You should be able to use the map as a prompt for a presentation you might make to colleagues.

To check the logic, many organisations add arrows showing the key connections between objectives. Again, avoid too many arrows.

Objectives are statements of outcome you place on the map. They provide answers to the drivers you created in **Step 4**. They are not actions. So 'Improve our customer journey' is an objective, but 'Buy a new database' is not. 'Reduce HIV infection among men' is an objective, but 'Give condoms to sex workers' is not. 'Engage government in the importance of our industry' is an objective, but 'Hire a PR firm to lobby for us' is not.

You want to end up with between two and five objectives for each perspective. If you have too many, it suggests you are not focusing on the vital few. And too few may mean the map is far too general.

Finally, it is normal to assign an owner to each objective to ensure some part of the organisation/team, or some senior individual, is held accountable for its achievement.

Call to action

- Can you answer the four key perspective questions in a simple and understandable way?
- Can you clearly articulate what the 10–15 key objectives are for your strategy map?
- Are you clear on the how/why logic? Can you explain the logical flow of ideas between each perspective?
- Take the map and begin to think about how to operationalise it – how to make it happen.

Step **10**

Maintain momentum: turning ideas into action

After reading this step you will be able to:

- Understand how to measure the success of your strategy
- Feel confident turning ideas into action using the three Ms
- Identify steps in creating an action plan
- Know how to involve others in delivering a strategy.

Developing a dieting strategy is easy . . . so why is losing weight so hard?

Think about losing weight. It is relatively easy to come up with a diet plan – eat fewer than 1,500 calories a day, try the 5/2 diet, go Atkins, give up drinking, etc. Any of these will work, if applied systematically.

So why is it so hard to keep up momentum on a diet? To succeed you need three Ms:

1. **Metrics:** you need data that tells you you are making progress in the right direction. For a successful diet strategy you need to know that you are losing weight and/or that your waistline is shrinking.

2. **Motivation:** you need some incentives and commitment to keep going, especially when things seem to be going wrong. For a successful diet strategy you need a reward like a new suit or a new dress when you succeed.

3. **Movement:** you need a specific action plan with time and tasks all organised in sequence. For a successful diet strategy you need to take specific action – actually give up bread or crisps or really go to the gym every week.

Let us work through these three Ms in relation to business strategy.

Metrics: make yourself a scorecard

In **Step 9** we talked about a scorecard as a way to track whether you are achieving your objectives. (This could be based on the strategy map you also created in **Step 9**.) To make sure you are succeeding, you need to ensure you are tracking the right things – you need good indicators.

Indicators are the concrete metrics to track the impact of activities you undertake to deliver your objectives. (For example, the number of complaints you receive is a measure – or indicator – of customer dissatisfaction. Be careful, though, as this measurement thing can be tricky. Against the obvious logic, companies with really good customer care tend to get more complaints as their customers know their complaints will be heard and dealt with. That is why complaints can also be a measure of customer satisfaction.)

 Beware trying to measure too many things.

You actually probably only need one or two key indicators for each objective to measure progress. This will ensure you stay focused on the most important measures. Too many measures will confuse you or slow you down as you try to take – unnecessary – remedial action on a whole range of issues.

So, you do not need to have information on all aspects of a car's functioning to make a successful journey. But you do probably need to know some key things, like how much petrol you have got and your speed. These are the key things that let you know if you are going to get to your destination at the time you expect. And, for your successful diet plan, you do not need to know everything about your body's metabolism or the exact calories of every meal – maybe just tracking the key measures of weight and waist will guide what you should or should not eat.

There are two types of indicator: lead and lag.

1. **A lead indicator** is what you measure to determine whether you are heading in the right direction to achieve the objective or outcome.

2. **A lag indicator** measures whether you have achieved the objective. The implication is that it will take some time – the cycle time lag – until the objective is achieved.

Look at the following example, related to the objective to lose eight kilos to look great on the beach in three months' time.

Metric	Purpose	Weight example
Lead indicator	To measure the early results that show you are heading in the right direction	Reduce daily calorie intake to below 1,500 calories Increase the number of workouts

Metric	Purpose	Weight example
Lag indicator	To measure how successful you are being in achieving the objective	This is normally a measure of the result: • kilos lost or • waist size reduced
Cycle time	This measures how long between the lead and the lag indicator to show success	You are unlikely to lose weight on a daily basis. That is why slimming clubs suggest a weekly weigh-in. This is a reasonable cycle period to track impact
Target	This is the specific outcome you want in a fixed period. (This can be the same as the overall objective but often it is a subset measured on a monthly, quarterly or even annual basis)	You might be aiming to lose a kilo a week over eight weeks – total eight kilos. The final month is a stabilisation month

Indicators define what will be measured to assess achievement of an objective. A target defines how much improvement is required over a specific period of time.

Some indicators are easy to measure – amount of extra sales income, number of new customers acquired, number of new products rolled out, etc. Others are difficult – staff motivation, customer response to brand, changes in attitude, etc.

When you cannot measure the impact of your objective directly, you need to use an analogue metric. This is a metric that suggests whether or not you are being successful. You could argue that level of staff absences is an analogue indicator for motivation. And you could argue that lack of customer churn is an indicator of brand loyalty. But you need to treat these with caution.

The cycle time – the length of time between the lead and lag indicator – is also important. In some cases, such as loyalty to a car manufacturer, the cycle time can be a number of years, since most people do not change their car very often. In other cases – such as whether your Twitter campaign goes viral – the cycle time can be as little as a day. So, when you are making an investment or planning decision, you need to be clear about over what period it is reasonable to decide that the objective is or is not being delivered.

 To see a practical example of how metrics make a difference, go to:

www.thebusinessgym.net

Case study

Customer care

Here is an example based on a broadband cable company that decides to launch a customer care programme to improve profitability and sell added-value services. They might choose the following lead and lag indicators:

Lead indicator	Estimated cycle time	Lag indicator
Number of customers signed up to annual direct debit payment	12 months	Retention/attrition levels improved at the end of 12 months
Number of customers indicating they would happily recommend a friend	3 months	Time for customer referral programme maturing and delivering net results
Number of additional offerings – mobiles, films, etc. – reviewed on website	6 months	Number of additional offerings adopted by customers and used for 3+ months

 **Exercise**

Begin by choosing one of your objectives that you are keen to achieve. As in **Step 9**, these might relate to:

- a specific profit or sales goal you have
- a customer acquisition or retention goal
- a new product development goal.

Now fill in the following table:

Objective:			
Lead indicator	**Lag indicator**	**Cycle time**	**Target**

Motivation

As in our weight loss example, it is essential that you look for ways to maintain momentum when trying to implement a strategy. See the quote below from Rosabeth Moss Kanter, Harvard Professor. Her argument is that many initiatives just take a long time to implement – especially when they are difficult. So success is not always easy or obvious. And, as in examples earlier in the book, it can take a long time to get things right – remember that Jeff Bezos and his shareholders waited 10 years for a profit at Amazon.

'Everything looks like a failure in the middle.'

Rosabeth Moss Kanter,
Harvard Business School Professor

So, the secrets of maintaining motivation are to:

- set really clear metrics and achievable targets to show if the positive trend is positive enough. And, if not, then think about whether to pivot (see **Challenge 4**)
- make sure key stakeholders get appropriate information – good or bad – regularly and in a form they want. Do not try hiding bad news in the hope it will get better – that is the mistake Nick Leeson made and he ended up bringing down Barings Bank in 1995. If the metrics show bad news, do not get depressed – try to work out why
- agree to give yourself a reward of some sort – for a personal target try a nice bottle of wine, a meal out or something else – when you achieve a specific target or milestone that indicates you are en route to success. A business target might involve a bonus.

Movement

The final element needed is movement – by which we mean taking practical action to turn the strategy into a real plan. This is the action or implementation plan outlined in **Step 9**.

There are many different ways to make a plan, but the easiest is, probably, a simple Gantt chart.

A Gantt chart is a project-planning tool in the form of a bar chart. Although now common, these charts were considered revolutionary when they were first brought in. Henry Gantt developed it in the early 20th century. It is claimed it transformed the USA's ability to deliver ships and materials to Europe as part of the effort to support the Allied Powers during the First World War.

The chart consists of three elements:

- **Tasks:** these are specific chunks of any project – so brief the marketing agency, design the campaign, print the brochures, etc.
- **Time:** for each of these tasks you need to know how long they will take – and in what sequence they need to be done.

- **Talent:** finally, you need to know who to have available to help – who is on the team to deliver the strategy and what abilities they have.

Below you can see a very simple example of a Gantt chart laid out for a new sales initiative. It is clear what each task is, who is responsible and when each task has to start and stop.

Task	Talent	Time											
		Jan	Feb	Mar	Apr	May	Jun	Jul	Aug	Sep	Oct	Nov	Dec
analyse results	JB				▓								
brief agency	BR			▓									
research	CS	▓											
develop options	AC		▓	▓									
agreed plan	JMcN					▓							
launch sales	CS								▓	▓	▓	▓	
review meeting	BR				▓								▓

Exercise

Think about a strategic initiative that you would like to get under way. Make a Gantt chart to show how you could progress it.

- Begin by listing all the tasks that have to be done to complete this project. Make all the tasks about the same level of granularity – so no task should be much bigger or smaller than the others.

- Next list the team – the talent – that you have available to help or that needs to be consulted for approval. Do you have any talent missing? Do you have enough people on the team?

- Now put the tasks onto the timeline in Excel. (There is specialist project-planning software, but Excel is normally fine for simple projects.) Make sure you are clear on the sequence and when specific activities start and stop.

Call to action

- Do you have a clear plan of action to get your strategic initiative under way? If not, get one. Even a dream needs a deadline!

- Are you clear on the metrics that will allow you to know whether you are succeeding? (And what will tell you you are failing?) Have you made sure you have metrics that are relevant to key stakeholders?

- Have you put in place some momentum milestones – that is, rewards for yourself or others to keep going with the project?

- Are you clear on the movement schedule? Do you have enough talent on board to keep this project going?

Part 2

10 strategy skills in action

Skill 1   Entering the dragon's den: pitching your idea

Skill 2   Transmitting on WIFM: the world's favourite radio station

Skill 3   Creating a burning platform: explaining difficult choices

Skill 4   Absolutely fabulous: planning strategy PR

Skill 5   Think, feel, do: getting your message across

Skill 6   Creating your strategy A Team: putting together talent

Skill 7   Meeting the black swan: thinking the unthinkable

Skill 8   Resistance is futile: overcoming the 5Cs

Skill 9   Strategic swimming: are you like a shark or a whale?

Skill 10   Strategy stylist: keeping up with fashionable gurus

Entering the dragon's den: pitching your idea

Having the idea is only the start of your strategic journey. You need to know who can make the decision to back your idea and then pitch it to them. Your mechanism for doing this may depend on the formal structures or the culture of your company. Generally, there are two main options – pitching to a group or pitching one to one.

> **Dilbert to Dogbert:** *My invention will turn people into mindless sheep.*
>
> **Dogbert to Dilbert:** *I'm curious how you'll know it works. I assume it's mostly a cosmetic change.*
>
> Scott Adams, *Dilbert*
> © 2002 United Feature Syndicate, Inc.

Entering the dragon's den

Your company may have a formal process for taking forward ideas. If they do, it is basically a good process, even if it can feel quite life threatening. In this case, you need to make three moves to make sure you are ready to enter.

- **Move 1: begin with them.** Start by thinking about the people you are going to pitch to. What are they like? What do you know about them? What are their interests and biases? Do they have a preference for new ideas or established ideas? Do they like ideas where they can add value and contribute or do they prefer ideas that are fully formed that they can simply sanction or agree to? Make a little profile of each person you may be pitching to. Try to decide in advance who may be positive towards your idea and who may be negative.

- **Move 2: shape it.** You need to organise your pitch so that you can express it in one line, in 30 seconds or 10 minutes. You may also need to have different versions of the pitch that will engage different dragons. These versions, especially the shorter ones, do not have to tell the whole story, but they do need to be sufficiently engaging to make people ask more questions. In the box below are some nice examples of film pitches, taken from the idea of the elevator pitch where you try to get in the lift with the famous producer and you have from floor 1 to floor 7 to sell your idea.

- **Move 3: talk in headlines.** In their book *Made to Stick*, the Heath brothers highlight a great example of this from the film *The Shipping News*. There is an exchange between the protagonist, who is learning how to write for a local newspaper, and his publisher:

Publisher: It's finding the centre of your story, the beating heart of it, that's what makes a reporter. You have to start by making up some headlines. You know: short, punchy, dramatic headlines.
Now, have a look [pointing at dark clouds gathering in the sky over the ocean]. What do you see? Tell me the headline.

Protagonist: HORIZON FILLS WITH DARK CLOUDS?

Publisher: IMMINENT STORM THREATENS VILLAGE.

Protagonist: But what if no storm comes?

Publisher: VILLAGE SPARED FROM DEADLY STORM.

To succeed in securing attention, you need to be able to reframe what your idea is in a simple and powerful way.

Your company is much more likely to be impressed by – and, more importantly, to remember – a smart and accurate one-line pitch summary.

What is your one-line pitch?

Elevator pitches

People in the film industry are famous for their short attention span, but being able to make massive strategic decisions really quickly. Below are a couple of examples of film elevator pitches.

- *Speed:* 'Die Hard on a bus.'
- *Alien:* 'Jaws on a spaceship.'

The one-to-one pitch

Sometimes, you are not facing a group but an individual who can choose to support your project – or not. Job one clearly is to get a meeting with this person. Once you are face to face with the potential project sponsor, you need to use the 5R sequence to help you get ready:

1. **Research:** if you are about to see a senior manager, find out as much as you can about them, their needs and their interests. What kind of projects have they backed in the past? Who can you talk to who has worked with them and can offer you some insight into their preferences? Do they like big picture concepts? Or do they prefer you to tell the story? You can find lots of anecdotes about what always works. But, actually, what works depends on the person to whom you are pitching and you need to be flexible in your approach.

2. **Rapport:** assuming you have managed to get into a room – or even an elevator – with the key individual, you need to build rapport with them. Rapport can involve matching body language, tone and language at a deep level. But, on a less complex level, you may want at least to show similarity, e.g. experiences that are similar to theirs. (So did they start out as a junior manager and work up by pitching ideas? Did they have a breakthrough notion that was hard to get accepted at one point and then find an important backer?) Do not be afraid to build on similarities.

3. **Reveal:** after building some rapport, you need to roll out or reveal your idea. Think carefully about how you want to do this. And make sure you rehearse and practise in your bedroom or the bathroom so you can deliver a perfectly formed roll out. This is also a time for passion and confidence – a good idea put across weakly will fail.

   Do not try to tell your whole story at once!

   Give them a taste of the potential and then offer to back up your idea with more detailed spreadsheets, narrative or whatever they need. Even if you are in a full pitch meeting, do not ramble on and on, hoping to gain approval through submission. Start with a brief 60-second overview pitch and then move to a 5–10 minute presentation that provides more detail.

4. **Response:** an effective pitch means listening as well as talking. It is important to pause between key ideas and look for a reaction. Ask if there are any further questions or if anything is unclear. Pay close attention to the response you get: excited and enthusiastic or sceptical and unconvinced? Pay close attention to them and what their verbal and non-verbal signs are telling you. If you get a positive response, or even just not a negative one, then move on.

5. **Request:** what do you want from this person? Do you want them to present your idea further up the hierarchy? Do you want them to authorise some seed capital or a whole project? Do you want them to encourage you to develop the idea further? You may want to have a range of requests available so that you can frame this based on the response you get to the reveal.

Get ready for the killer question

Killer questions are flaws in your idea – or at least the challenges – for which you do not have a good answer. Your passion is a good thing and your commitment and confidence add value. But these positives may blindside you to some of the drawbacks or difficulties that are implicit in your project.

Ideally, you should anticipate any killer questions and have the answers ready. A good way to do this is to get a friend to play devil's advocate and get them to ask the most challenging questions that they can. These may include:

- **'What if . . . ' questions:** ones that assume things could go wrong. 'How would you deal with a change in the market/ competitors stealing your idea/a change in financial regulations/changing demographics?'

- **'You've assumed . . . ' questions:** ones that look for the underlying assumptions in your proposal. They are connected to 'what if' questions, but are more concerned with the embedded logic of the project. For example, 'You've assumed that interest rates remain the same/you've assumed that the Chinese market continues to grow/you've assumed that young people are interested in that kind of entertainment.'

- **'I heard that . . . ' questions:** this brings in a left-field piece of information or even an anecdote designed to challenge some part of your idea. You should, of course, be familiar with all these issues. But, if not, listen to what they have to say and offer to come back with a detailed response in 24 hours.

Whatever happens, when you get a killer question, do not panic or get into a row with a potential sponsor. Challenging them will, almost certainly, not lead to a positive outcome. Take careful note of the question and, if you have a good answer, respond in a calm, measured, reasonable way. If you do not know the answer, offer to go away and think it through and come back to them. Write down what they said. Showing that you are committed to handling challenge is a good business discipline. It fits with your strategic image. (To work more on you as a brand look at **Challenge 2: #me: how to develop powerful personal branding**.)

Transmitting on WIFM: the world's favourite radio station

Whether you work in a big company or a relatively small one, there will be people who are interested in your strategic idea and people whose support you need to make it happen. We talked about the idea of stakeholders in **Step 1**.

 It is essential that you are clear who these individuals are, what their relative importance is and what you need from them.

To do this, imagine you are running a radio station – the world's favourite radio station, WIFM (what's in it for me?). Your audience for WIFM are the stakeholders who can help make or break your strategic idea.

Key jobs

Job 1

Job 1 is to make a list of the individuals – or even groupings – you think you need to involve. Think about both internal and external stakeholders. (Look back at **Step 1** for the definition.) As a reminder, stakeholders can range pretty widely, as shown in the following table.

Any of these people could be vital to the success of any strategy. It is worth brainstorming who might be important at the start.

Internal	External
Shareholders	Regulators
Chair of the board	Customers
Board members	Suppliers
Senior managers	Business partners
Team boss	Retailers
Team members	Distributors
Colleagues in other departments	Channel partners

Job 2

Job 2 is to be really clear about *why* you think you need to have them involved – what can they bring to the party, what kind of sanction or sign off do you need from them?

Fill in the following tables:

Internal stakeholder	Why do you need them to be involved?	What do you want from them?	What are their concerns?

External stakeholder	Why do you need them to be on board?	What do you want them to get?	What are their concerns?

External stakeholder	Why do you need them to be on board?	What do you want them to get?	What are their concerns?

Job 3

Job 3 is to identify what the key issues are that each internal stakeholder wants to have addressed. Probably, the easiest way to do this is to think about the three questions that the strategic idea needs to answer in order for them to engage with it.

Job 4

Job 4 is to think of a way to excite interest in and enthusiasm for your idea. Remember that the more senior people probably receive many different communications – by email, in meetings, through telephone calls, etc. So it is important you make sure your idea really stands out in their mental inbox.

Here are two possible ways to do this, both of which are meant to be slightly fun exercises.

 Create a knockout email headline

Imagine you have to send an email to this person and they will have time to open only 10 emails that day. How can you make sure your email is one of those 10? What would make your email subject heading stand out – 'Copy of strategic plan idea for your review'? Does that grab your interest? Do you think it would grab anyone else's?

How about something catchier, like: 'Solving the problem of the under 16s market' or 'Three options to improve our profitability'. We guess that either of these subject headings is more likely to attract attention.

Answer their questions up front

An alternative approach is to tackle the three key questions you believe that person would like to have answered before they have asked them. Put them in the executive summary of your document or in the email. This will then make reading about the detail of your idea much easier.

Think about two directors – one the finance director and the other the HR director.

The finance director may ask:

- How risky is this likely to be?
- Will it offer a good RoI?
- Are there cheaper alternatives?

However, the HR director may ask:

- Will this create disruption among staff?
- Will there be a training or coaching need?
- How many people will be involved?

You need to answer these questions somewhere in the text of your strategy or you will not be transmitting on the world's favourite radio station, WIFM.

Creating a burning platform: explaining difficult choices

Urgent and important

For people to adopt a strategy that will mean radical change, they need to feel it is both *important* and *urgent*. How do you convey that sense? Unfortunately, it is likely to involve creating a pain message – and a burning platform is a very specific, uncompromising kind of message.

> 'Orchestrating pain messages throughout the institution is the first step in developing organizational commitment to (major) change.'
>
> Rosabeth Moss Kanter,
> former editor, *Harvard Business Review*

Burning platforms are very powerful drivers of strategic change. They are what happens when:

- there is a real and immediate crisis
- there is a limited number of difficult and challenging choices
- each choice is irreversible
- each choice has a high risk of failure.

The phrase comes from a real incident dating back to 6 July 1988. On that date, the Piper Alpha oilrig in the North Sea exploded, as a result of failing to check some simple systems that had worked faultlessly for the previous decade. The explosion, in turn, caused a massive fire. 167 men died – the largest number ever killed in an offshore accident.

The scale of the blast was immense. The flames from the blaze shot 90 metres in the air and, apparently, could be seen 100 km away.

At first, the workers locked themselves in a room in part of the rig, hoping the fire would burn out or emergency systems would kick in. Eventually, three men, realising this would not work, made it to the edge of the platform and stood staring into one of the world's coldest and roughest seas. They had two choices – to stay where they were and hope to be rescued from the flames or to jump into the freezing water and risk almost certain death from hypothermia. Two men chose to jump – and they lived, despite being terribly injured, thanks to a rescue operation mounted by sea. The man who chose to stay sadly perished, as helicopters failed to make it in time.

That story contains some powerful learning about the need to respond positively and proactively to serious strategic challenges. It also offers a clue about how to communicate about such challenges.

First, there is the idea of the unacceptable option of staying the same. The man who stayed on the rig died, essentially, because he waited for someone else to help him.

 Staying the same – not going through the change – and hoping things will get better is to risk probable failure.

Second is the message that sometimes radical, risky change is essential, if painful. Against the odds, the two who jumped survived, though they broke their legs in the process. It hurt, but the action they took gave them the very slight advantage they needed. Above all, they took action.

A burning platform is a situation so serious that there *has* to be action.

Case study

Nokia's burning platform

A subsequent famous example of a burning platform was that experienced by Nokia in 2011. Though it had once seemed invincible, dominating the market, other companies – Apple,

Google and Samsung – had seriously eroded Nokia's share. The CEO, Stephen Elop, sent a memo to all staff telling them that if the company was to survive, it had no choice but to join forces with Microsoft and move its products over from its own – superior – operating system to Windows 8.

His argument? Staying the same would not work. Teaming up with Microsoft was not a great choice, but it was a positive choice and, unlike the company's present predicament, it offered some hope of success. (Though, as we now know, it did not work. Microsoft closed Nokia; burning platforms are risky and cannot always be escaped.)

How to apply the model

What is the burning platform in your company that requires urgent and courageous attention? What are the negative consequences of not changing? What should you do, even if it is risky?

Decide on the strategic change you want to promote, accepting that often people will change only when faced with a pressing challenge with potentially negative consequences.

- Identify one choice, describe the challenges and suggest the possible advantages to taking risky action.
- Describe staying the same as a *worse* choice, outlining the greater difficulties it presents and the certainty of failure.

Use the following table to outline your strategic proposition. Remember to be clear who you are trying to sell this to.

Think of a strategic change you want to create in your team, department or company – what is the burning platform message?	
The high-risk action choice	The even worse static choice

Absolutely fabulous: planning strategy PR

A PR strategy . . . for your strategy

Strategies need social momentum to gain traction. Often, this momentum is more to do with PR – public relations – than the actual quality of the thinking underpinning them.

So, once you have your strategy, you may need to organise a PR campaign across your team, your department or even the company to ensure it is accepted and actioned.

Decide on your target audience

We have already discussed the need to identify the key target audience for any strategic communication. You simply may want to review the analysis you conducted in **Skill 2** to establish who those priority audiences are.

Your list of key PR targets might include people who you need to have on board because of their seniority, their knowledge or their ability to sign off your ideas. This could include:

- senior managers
- colleagues
- team leaders
- finance managers.

Whoever you identify, you should be clear on who they are and why you need them on board.

Once you have your list, you need to establish their relative priority:

A = a key audience: they must be on board

B = a secondary audience: good to have engaged

C = nice to have along: but not essential.

You then need to make sure your efforts are targeted at the key A audience. Having a lot of Cs on board is not useful. It is like the hangers-on party. Make sure you have a VIP section of As.

The law of the few

You now have a list of the people with obvious structural power. But how do you reach them – especially when some are at a significant distance from you? And how do you make sure your idea has a positive buzz about it? You could organise stunts – but these can be high risk and may backfire.

Part of the answer is you also need to pay attention to people with social power. This is a phenomenon described by Malcolm Gladwell in his book *The Tipping Point,* which describes how ideas become viral and gain traction. Specifically, he describes it as 'that magic moment when an idea, trend, or social behavior crosses a threshold, tips, and spreads like wildfire'. He cites examples as diverse as the runaway sales of Hush Puppies shoes in the mid-1990s and the remarkable drop in the crime rate in New York City. He argues that a major factor in these viral successes was the active presence of three groups with social power:

- **Connectors are the individuals in any community:** maybe a city, business, department, team – who know large numbers of people and who enjoy making introductions and connections. Usually, they know people outside their own specific discipline and across a range of social, cultural and professional circles. These people, Gladwell says, 'are full of curiosity, self-confidence, sociability, and energy'. By selling them your idea and bringing them on board initially, you are guaranteed your idea will get out across the company.
- **Mavens are what Gladwell describes as 'information specialists':** more specifically, 'people we rely upon to

connect us with new information'. They gather knowledge and information about markets and trends and they like to share it with others. Mavens start 'word-of-mouth epidemics' because of their knowledge combined with social skills. Gladwell states, 'Mavens are really information brokers, sharing and trading what they know.' So, a Maven will help check out your idea – and their backing will convince others that your idea has traction.

- **Salespeople are Gladwell's final cluster:** these people are persuaders – socially engaging and charming and often with sound business skills. This mix of skills means others tend to want to agree with them and salespeople are keen to reinforce their own position and status by sharing ideas they think have value. It is useful to have some salespeople on your side. They will make it their job to sell your idea.

Simple sales messages – learning from Leonardo da Vinci

Your strategy probably needs to be underpinned by spreadsheets, slides, Gantt charts, etc. to give it logical credibility. But logic is

Source: photo by Jakub Krechowicz

not everything. You may also want to think about the overall communications message itself. Below is a letter written by Leonardo da Vinci seeking employment with the Duke of Milan. It lists 10 reasons why the Duke should hire him. (Notice that da Vinci mentions only the thing he really wants to do – make art – *after* his 10 reasons. Everything else is targeted at the Duke and his interests.)

> *'Having, most illustrious lord, seen and considered the experiments of all those who pose as masters in the art of inventing instruments of war, and finding that their inventions differ in no way from those in common use, I am emboldened, without prejudice to anyone, to solicit an appointment of acquainting your Excellency with certain of my secrets.*
>
> 1. *I can construct bridges which are very light and strong and very portable, with which to pursue and defeat the enemy; and others more solid, which resist fire or assault, yet are easily removed and placed in position; and I can also burn and destroy those of the enemy.*
>
> 2. *In case of a siege I can cut off water from the trenches and make pontoons and scaling ladders and other similar contrivances.*
>
> 3. *If by reason of the elevation or the strength of its position a place cannot be bombarded, I can demolish every fortress if its foundations have not been set on stone.*
>
> 4. *I can also make a kind of cannon which is light and easy of transport, with which to hurl small stones like hail, and of which the smoke causes great terror to the enemy, so that they suffer heavy loss and confusion.*
>
> 5. *I can noiselessly construct to any prescribed point subterranean passages either straight or winding, passing if necessary underneath trenches or a river.*
>
> 6. *I can make armoured wagons carrying artillery, which shall break through the most serried ranks of the enemy, and so open a safe passage for his infantry.*
>
> 7. *If occasion should arise, I can construct cannon and mortars and light ordnance in shape both ornamental and useful and different from those in common use.*

8. *When it is impossible to use cannon I can supply in their stead catapults, mangonels, trabocchi, and other instruments of admirable efficiency not in general use – in short, as the occasion requires I can supply infinite means of attack and defence.*

9. *And if the fight should take place upon the sea I can construct many engines most suitable either for attack or defence and ships which can resist the fire of the heaviest cannon, and powders or weapons.*

10. *In time of peace, I believe that I can give you as complete satisfaction as anyone else in the construction of buildings both public and private, and in conducting water from one place to another.*

I can further execute sculpture in marble, bronze or clay, also in painting I can do as much as anyone else, whoever he may be.

Moreover, I would undertake the commission of the bronze horse, which shall endure with immortal glory and eternal honour the auspicious memory of your father and of the illustrious house of Sforza.

And if any of the aforesaid things should seem to anyone impossible or impracticable, I offer myself as ready to make trial of them in your park or in whatever place shall please your Excellency, to whom I commend myself with all possible humility.'

Leonardo da Vinci (Incidentally, da Vinci got the job and kept it for 16 years, until the French invaded the city and captured his employer.)

Think, feel, do: getting your message across

Rational and emotional

To sell a strategy effectively, you need to *communicate* the plan that you or your planning team has developed in a powerful and simple way. This needs to be *rational* and relate to your drivers – see **Step 4** – but it must also go beyond that to become a positive and engaging *message.* This message must be communicated constantly, consistently and across many different channels to ensure it reaches and is understood by as many people as possible, including the key stakeholders discussed in **Skill 2**.

Your strategy need not be fully worked out in every detail and you may even want people to have a hand in developing it, but there must be enough of a plan for people to orientate themselves towards it.

Making your plan powerful

To make your plan powerful, you should consider carefully how to shape it for communication. One way is to organise it through three elements – *think, feel* and *do* (TFD).

Think	Feel	Do
What do you want people to think, know or understand?	How do you want people to feel or respond? (Or how do you feel?)	What specific action do you want people to take?

- **Think:** what will people *think, know* or *understand* in your strategy? This could relate to the facts – the benefits to customers, the advantages of the new structure, the development opportunities.

- **Feel:** how will people *feel* about this fact? What feeling or emotion – pride, happiness, excitement, etc. – do you want to generate?

- **Do:** what *action* or *actions* would you like people to take that will move the strategy on? How can they specifically contribute?

You need to consider whether the information is convincing and concrete enough. And whether the feeling you have identified is appropriate and strong enough and whether the action is specific and doable.

So, if you were the manager of a customer care helpline team, who needs to introduce some new approaches, you might say something similar to the examples shown in the following table.

Think	Feel	Do
'We've not been answering all calls to the helpline – one in four is being missed since we keep people hanging on.' 'We want to be sure that everyone who needs to contact us can always do so and be treated in a professional way.'	'I'm embarrassed that we've not been delivering the service our customers deserve. I guess you are, too.' 'I want to feel proud of the service we provide. And I'm excited by the way the new approach will help us deliver 100 per cent satisfaction.'	'We need to introduce new working practices to ensure that we answer all calls in time.' 'I need you to be open to some new ways of working I've devised. And to come up with your own suggestions for further improvement.'

You can think of this model as a way to frame your elevator pitch – see **Skill 1**. The message should be expressed as simply as possible so that it is capable of being repeated – accurately – by others.

Think about a strategic change you want to make. Make notes to help below.

Think
Feel
Do

Make it imaginative!

It is not enough to *have* TFD – you need to share it in an engaging way to really have an impact.

- When one big UK charity planned their merger with another, they organised a whole campaign around the film empire *Star Wars* with a guiding message that anything was possible with the coalition tackling the Big Evil of failure.

- An enterprising CEO attached his vision message to a KitKat biscuit and left it on all employees' desks overnight. His message was 'take a break and read the vision'. What could have been a boring memo turned into an event.

- A small business owner arranged to have mugs done with the company vision and values printed on them. This meant that every time staff had a cup of tea or coffee they were reminded about the vision and values.

What can you do to share your vision in an unusual way? How will you make it engaging/visceral?

Creating your strategy A Team: putting together talent

> 'Never doubt that a small group of thoughtful, committed citizens can change the world. Indeed it is the only thing that ever has.'
>
> Margaret Mead, American author and cultural anthropologist

What is a strategy team?

Unless you are super smart and super connected, you will need to work with a group of people to help you develop and possibly, even, deliver any strategy. And you yourself may, of course, be asked to be part of a strategic project team organised by a more senior colleague.

This group does not need to know all the answers. It does, though, need to accept responsibility and have authority to develop a strategy and possibly, even, guide it through. Its members are likely to be mostly internal, but it might also include some external stakeholders, such as suppliers or even customers.

Who should be on your A team? What skills and talents do you need in the team to plan and deliver the strategy?

Create your A Team

The A Team, from the 2010 film, based on the cult 1980s TV series, contained a number of different skills, which helped make them successful in pulling off the most amazing results. Hannibal had a strong grasp of planning; Murdoch was brilliant at engineering and fixing; Face was charming and communicative; and Mr T. provided muscle and – when necessary – threat. Individually, they were not particularly effective. As a team they were unbeatable.

In putting together your strategy team, think about applying the same broad approach – bringing together individuals with different talents who together can help shape and deliver your ideas.

It is tempting to make up a team of friends and allies – they like you, you like them. But, you may not end up with the best team to deliver the result you are looking for. Rather, you need to be clear about the specific skillsets and mindsets that you need in order to develop or deliver your strategic plan. These might include some of the following:

Skillsets	Mindsets
• Marketing	• Creative
• Sales	• Critical
• Communications	• Ambitious
• Finance	• Driven

Talent tweet

One effective way to think about who you would like to have on board is to write a talent tweet – a 140-character message that conveys the sort of person or people you would like to have to help you with your strategy. You could even actually tweet it to colleagues in the company.

Use this simple communication as a way to engage other people in helping with your project. The discipline of the 140 characters is useful to focus the mind.

Mission, mandate and membership

Once you have selected your strategy team, you need to get them focused by giving them a specific mission, mandate and membership. See the following table for some questions to help you construct this important three-part project description.

Mission: What is the overarching team purpose?   What will success mean?   How will success be measured?   Is there a specific goal? A deadline?
Mandate: What is the scope of the project? And what is not in scope or off limits?   In what circumstances can this change?   Who can sign off changes?
Membership: Who should be involved?   How big should the team be? And where should they be drawn from?   What skillsets and mindsets should they have? (See above.)

Having your A Team is an important step on the way to making progress with your strategic journey.

Meeting the black swan: thinking the unthinkable

Black swan events are sudden, dramatic, high-impact events that make a massive difference. Such events might include the 9/11 terrorist attacks in NYC, the global crash in 2008 or, even, on a more positive side, the invention of the internet. When such events happen in business they can cause massive disruption.

Black swan is a phrase popularised by the economist Nassim Taleb in his book *The Black Swan* (2007). Originally, he focused on financial events, but has since expanded the idea to look at broader political and social events. The idea of the black swan originally comes from a quotation by Roman writer Juvenal. Juvenal talks about black swans as being mythical and improbable. And, in fact, they were not known to exist until the explorer Willem de Vlamingh spotted them in Australia in 1697.

According to Taleb, a real black swan has three key characteristics:

1. The event should be significant and have a major impact.
2. The event should be unexpected.
3. In retrospect, the event probably was predictable.

The Scottish poet, Robert Burns, famously captured the possibility of things going horribly wrong in an unexpected way in his poem *To a Mouse*. The context, if you are unfamiliar with Burns, is that a ploughman destroys the nest of a mouse in a field. He stops and notices the small creature looking scared and puzzled amid the debris of the nest. The famous lines capture the impact of a black swan:

> *'The best-laid schemes o' mice an' men*
>
> *Gang aft agley, [often go wrong]*

An' lea'e us nought but grief an' pain,

For promis'd joy!'

The mice and men theme was picked up by Douglas Adams and reversed in *The Hitchhiker's Guide to the Galaxy*. There the mice commission planet Earth as an experiment to find the answer to the ultimate question of life, the universe and everything. When their plans go wrong and the earth is accidentally destroyed by a Vogon spacecraft making an intergalactic highway, sadly they comment that 'the best laid plans of mice' do not always work out.

In the less esoteric world of business, major black swan events might include:

- a sudden scandal – perhaps the chief executive being involved in a sex or drugs issue that causes shareholder confidence to fall
- a technological breakthrough that means that the current way of operating becomes impractical
- a takeover by another company that leads to a dramatic change in the scale and scope of the business.

Even in your own team, the sudden departure of your team boss or an unexpected opportunity for a massive promotion could be a black swan.

A black swan event is not confined to business – you could have one in your personal life. For example:

- you suffer an injury while skiing, which means you are immobile for a year
- you win the lottery and suddenly have money to do exactly what you want
- you are offered an amazing job in another country that you have never been to.

Whether the black swan is professional or personal, you need to develop some tactics to deal with it. A black swan is different from risk management. So, although you might take some precautions, when it hits – like it or not – it will have a transformational impact on your organisation or your life.

A key feature of a black swan event seems to be the level of the shock experienced by those involved. It can be the impact of this shock, rather than the traumatic nature of the event itself, that has the greatest negative consequences. For example:

- you feel too paralysed to respond and, as you delay response, the problem becomes even worse
- you feel you have to do *something* and so rush into inappropriate or ineffective action, without a real plan.

These responses, of course, are the worst possible ones when trying to deal with a very volatile situation where you need to be clear and calm in order to engage with what is happening.

If you have seen the film *Apollo 13* – based on the real-life incident – you will know that the three astronauts were faced with a black swan event when a critical battery caught fire. The resulting reduction in power in the spacecraft was going to lead to a slow cold death in outer space if they did not take action. It was important that everyone – the astronauts and the ground crew – remained calm, but they also needed to find an innovative solution as quickly as possible.

 You can see a clip from the film on YouTube here:

https://www.youtube.com/watch?v=C2YZnTL596Q

This illustrates a textbook positive approach to effective problem solving in a crisis.

Scientists on the ground were given equipment typical of things the astronauts could find on the stricken craft and told to work out a way to make a square filter fit into a round hole. They needed to abandon their structured systematic thinking and apply imagination – and duct tape – to come up with the answer.

Taleb has come up with a list of key principles to help you deal with a black swan event:

- **Assess the situation:** spend time taking stock and establishing the scale and scope of the challenge.
- **Look twice:** make sure you are clear what is *really* happening. Do not jump to conclusions.

- **Be confident:** go into the situation confident you will find a solution rather than nervous and overwhelmed.
- **Be innovative:** almost certainly, the thinking and techniques you have used to deal with previous situations will not help. Be innovative and open to new ideas.
- **Seek help:** do not be afraid to ask others for help. It is not a sign of weakness but of strength – and you may need new allies to help you.
- **Build persistence:** it is unlikely you will come up with the right solution first time – try lots of different approaches. And keep trying.

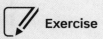 **Exercise**

Have a go at applying the black swan principles to an event that might happen in your personal life. You have broken both legs in a skiing accident and are immobile for the next six months, which means it is very difficult for you to go into work. Unfortunately, you are the lead on a really important project to launch a new product. Fill in your responses to the questions below:

Approach	Your response
Assess the situation: What are the overall implications? How serious are they?	
Look twice: What are some alternative ways to think about this? Are they + or −?	
Be confident: Notice how you feel. Adopt a positive attitude.	
Be innovative: Are there any new approaches you can think of?	
Seek help: Who can you turn to for help and advice?	

Approach	Your response
Build persistence: What other options do you have to try if this approach does not work?	

Now apply this same technique to a business issue. Think of a challenge that might come up in a project you are working on that would meet the three black swan criteria discussed at the beginning of this section. Answer the same five questions to address this challenge.

 In some ways, black swans can be thought of as career makers or career breakers. The key is to take advantage of them as well as you possibly can and, above all, *do not panic*.

Resistance is futile: overcoming the 5Cs

Responses to change

Inevitably, putting a strategy into place requires change. So, when you are planning how you are going to communicate your strategic ideas, it is important to understand that any organisational change will provoke different reactions in different people (though it is not absolutely necessary to adopt *Star Trek*'s Borg 'resistance is futile' hard line).

Let us say you have the opportunity to roll out a change across the department. As you finish addressing the departmental meeting, you see five basic responses. We call these the 5Cs of change.

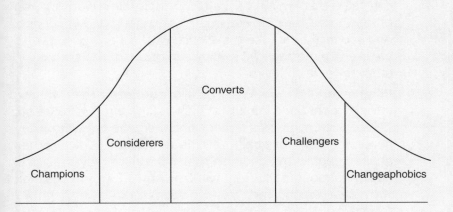

It is important to say this is a framework that offers a snapshot of views and people may move between categories at any point. When you are heading up a strategic change, your task is to get as many people as possible to move from the negative side of the curve to the positive. To do this, you need to understand:

- why people are in each category
- what you need to do to respond and help them move
- what the advantages and disadvantages are for each cluster.

Let us begin by describing how you might recognise each of the responses.

- **Champions** are, perhaps, 5–10 per cent of the total. They are the people who are prepared to stick their neck out and run with your idea. They crowd around you after your presentation on the strategy, smiling and shaking your hand.

- **Considerers** are 15–20 per cent of the total. They are the people who do not immediately respond positively, as they need a bit of time to reflect first. They will send you an email later in the day saying they think it is, basically, a good idea, having thought about it. Considerers follow either because they wish to emulate others or because, after a pause, they can see the advantages of the strategy.

- **Converts** are 30–40 per cent of the total. They are the biggest single group. They listen in silence to your presentation and can fall either way in terms of positivity or negativity. You probably find their silence quite intimidating and unnerving. And you might confuse the silence with negativity. Converts are likely to require solid evidence in favour of the strategy in order to come on board.

- **Challengers** are 15–20 per cent of the total. They will ask difficult questions initially and then . . . continue to do so. Their basic approach is to confront and to be awkward. They generally resist or challenge the new – not because they are bad people, but because they have a strongly analytical or critical approach. They will trawl for flaws in your plan with a fine toothcomb. This can seem like a lot of negative feedback.

- **Changeaphobics** are 5–10 per cent of the total. No matter how irrational their fears, they will not be convinced. Though they are generally few in number, they are still important in so far as they can slow down or even – in extreme circumstances – derail your strategy. They may not be vocal, but they will cause dissent or stir things. And they are, essentially, immovable. Changeaphobics are tough.

How to deal with the 5Cs

Each of the 5Cs requires a different approach from you as the person selling the strategic change.

Champions

Everyone likes the idea of champions – they are on your side. But you need to treat champions cautiously. They have advantages, no question, which include:

- providing you with support
- acting as advocates with other people.

But champions have disadvantages, too:

- They are, generally, champions of everything and might be similarly enthusiastic about your proposal to paint the office green. That can make them bad judges of what makes something fly. And they may give you a false impression of how well your proposal has gone down overall.
- As a result of this reputation, their endorsement might not be highly regarded by other people. In fact, their endorsement may work against you. (Think of Toad in *Wind of the Willows* – his constant enthusiasm is treated sceptically.)
- Their enthusiasm means they will not question you too closely and they are, therefore, likely to follow your ideas blindly without really thinking them through. This can be dangerous. For you and for them.

To deal with champions, give them something practical to do to absorb their energy. And be careful about using them as advocates for your strategy, as others may treat what they say with caution or even scepticism.

Considerers

Considerers are the ones who look around at the end of a briefing meeting to see who else is on board. They discuss your proposal with others before forming a judgement and, generally, look to a key opinion former or someone with social power for guidance. Considerers have their advantages:

- Giving you an accurate view of how your idea is being received.
- Their joining in is a sign you are making progress.
- Once committed, they will stay with you.

And considerers have some disadvantages, too:

- They come on board only if you convince the right trigger person – a team leader or CEO.
- They will not come on board immediately and that pause or gap may leave you feeling anxious (and others wondering if you are going to succeed).
- They may need reassurance on a very specific concern. For example, how the restructure that is part of the plan impacts on them or their team.

To bring these people on board, you need to identify key social influencers at various levels. Brief them in advance and they will encourage the considerers. (Remember trying to organise a party when you were at school? Once you had identified the most popular person and persuaded them to come, everyone else accepted their invitations.)

Converts

As the biggest single group in the 5Cs, converts have some advantages:

- Once you bring them on board, you know your proposal will be adopted.
- They tend to be slow to adopt a strategy that involves change or innovation, but they are equally slow to let it go. Once they are on board, you have momentum.

Converts also have their disadvantages:

- They take so long to come on board that an opportunity you wanted to seize is lost.

- You find your initiative loses momentum or focus, especially if you end up responding to a whole range of small issues that concerns them.

Think carefully about converts' concerns before launching your initiative. If you can answer them in advance, you will be able to bring them on board more quickly. Produce a list of FAQs and you should find that helps.

Challengers

Challengers ask difficult questions. They want to test your ideas to the limit and need careful handling. They have advantages, although these may not seem immediately apparent:

- Asking difficult questions that force you to check out your thinking or plan rather than assuming you are right.

- Asking questions on behalf of others, especially the converts. So, indirectly, you may be able to reassure them.

And challengers' disadvantages are:

- They can carry on asking difficult questions beyond the point at which it is useful. You need to be clear with them where the boundaries are.

- They ask questions on issues that you regard as inappropriate or that you think are too sensitive or not up for discussion.

When dealing with challengers, it is important you handle their queries fairly and evenly – however irritated you may feel – as others are watching. Think about your response. What are you committed to and what are you open to discuss? Be clear on this distinction. And also be clear what is 'off the agenda'.

Changeaphobics

Changeaphobics are difficult. They oppose your idea on principle and are intractably opposed. They do not do this from a sense of badness, but because they feel your plan is too high risk. Their only advantages are:

- If you are seen to deal with them honestly and fairly, you will gain brownie points from others who will perceive you as just and even-handed.
- They force you to consider how determined you are to implement your plan.

Changeaphobics' disadvantages are legion. Among them:

- They will do their best to stop your initiative.
- They will always be opposed to it.
- They can significantly lower morale among others.

 The harsh reality is you *have* to get changeaphobics out of the way as quickly as you can. Or you may need to help them to leave.

Work out your engagement plan. Think about the people you have to ask to adopt your strategy and their response to the change it will entail – and what you should do.			
Response cluster	**Who is in the cluster and how many?**	**What is their concern?**	**What tactic should you use?**
Champions			
Considerers			
Converts			
Challengers			
Changeaphobics			

Strategic swimming: are you like a shark or a whale?

Two approaches to the business ocean

The ocean is full of many creatures that have different lifestyles. Two interesting contrasting ones are sharks and whales.

1. Sharks tend to stay in a relatively defined area. They are aggressive predators fighting to survive. When a creature is vulnerable – think of the classic sailor-lost-at-sea film – sharks surround it and compete to get the largest chunk of their victim. Sharks live in a metaphorical *red ocean* environment.

2. Whales spend their days cruising the world's oceans. They are untroubled, by and large, by other creatures. They are at the top of the marine food chain, eating krill and not really competing directly with other creatures. Whales live in a metaphorical *blue ocean* environment.

You can face two similar choices when drafting a strategy: creating new customer demand in an uncontested market space – *blue ocean* – or competing head-to-head with other organisations for established customers in an existing industry – *red ocean*. (This model is based on *Blue Ocean Strategy,* an influential book written by W. Chan Kim and Renée Mauborgne.)

Each strategic approach requires a different mindset and skillset. Only blue ocean can offer high returns, but red ocean is safer. Most of the rest of the book is concerned with red ocean approaches – teaching you how to compete more effectively. **Skill 9** looks at how to think and plan for blue ocean.

An example of blue ocean is Apple's introduction of the tablet PC – creating a brand new category of device that millions of people now use. Or Cirque du Soleil's reimagining of circus performance as an event for adults rather than children, and without animals. Red ocean is the fight for market share between energy suppliers or the big supermarkets struggling to attract – and keep – customers.

Our talented colleague Angela Cluff is one of a handful of global experts on this model and has used it with a number of charity agencies to help them distinguish their offering. A good example is to help one agency distinguish itself in what is called the Pink Fog – that is the sheer number of agencies working on breast cancer issues in the UK. (How many can you name? Can you tell the difference between Breast Cancer Campaign and Breakthrough Breast Cancer?) It is bad enough that almost all of them use the colour pink and a ribbon motif to emphasise their commitment to this issue. So that creates a problem for donors – how do these charities distinguish themselves when they all offer a package of support, counselling and research?

 If you want to know more about the range of red ocean and blue ocean tools, you might find this download that Angela has written useful. To gain access, sign up at the following link:

www.managementcentre.co.uk/knowledgebase/ does-your-big-idea-look-red-or-blue

Should you choose blue or red?

So, blue ocean strategies are preferable in terms of return, but they are not always possible or practical. For a start, you need a properly big idea and then you are likely to need significant marketing and/or R&D spend to develop your idea. In a red ocean market, it is really clear what the key success factors are and you may simply be able to outspend/perform your rivals. The following table summarises the choice.

	Red ocean	Blue ocean
Market context	The category of existing and understood markets	The category of markets that do not exist or are undeveloped
Your strategic approach	• Compete by trading off value and cost – be cheaper/better value! • Watch the competition closely – counter any move they make • Understand the rules of the game – and work within them • Maximise share – accept that profits and growth shrink	• Be the only one so that you can provide value and maximise returns • Make the idea of competition irrelevant – be unique in category • Change the rules of the game – seek to disrupt them • Create a market – look for new customers or develop demand
What are the risks?	• Competition becomes unbearable – margins are too low, you have to exit • A larger competitor forces you from the market	• No one cares about your new idea – 'a gap in the market, but no market in the gap' • You run out of funds before you hit blue ocean

Blue ocean tools

There are as many as 16 tools to help you develop a blue ocean strategy. But perhaps the most immediately useful one is the Four Actions Framework. This encourages you to look at what you currently do, and then look for ways to:

1. Reduce factors and therefore cost.

2. Eliminate factors and therefore cost.

3. Raise standards without increasing cost.

4. Create standards that satisfy customers – again, with no increase in cost.

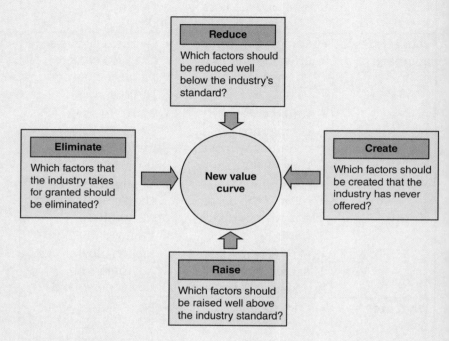

If you think that is a tough call, you are right – you are being asked to add value and reduce cost at the same time. Hard, but it can be done.

A classic example of this is the way The Body Shop first tackled the UK market for ethical cosmetics (see the following figure).

Think about the work you currently do or even the overall work of the company. Apply blue ocean thinking using the Four Actions Framework. Be radical!

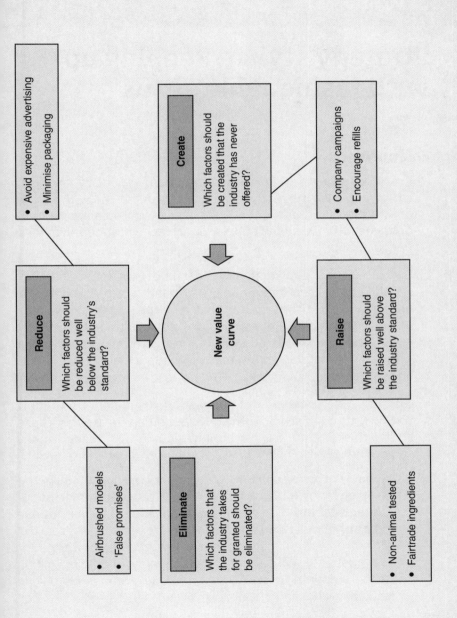

Strategy stylist: keeping up with fashionable gurus

Fashion sense

Everyone loves the idea of strategy and, especially, the very clever and wise gurus who produce big ideas. Sadly, the world of strategy is rather like the world of fashion. Ideas are in or out of vogue – they become popular or achieve great currency for a period of time.

Part of your job is to keep up to speed on what is hot and what is not. Luckily, there are a number of books written to help you understand what these gurus said, why their work is important and why you should – or should not – pay attention to it. To get you started, we have listed 11 pivotal gurus you should be familiar with and summarised in a few easily digestible lines their key ideas and why they are important.

Just to be clear, we are not suggesting you should try to bluff your way through an in-depth conversation on the back of these summaries. Rather, they will allow you to nod wisely or say something sensible over the water cooler or a flat white in Pret.

1. **Michael Porter:** at one time the highest-paid consultant in the world, charging $20,000 a day, Porter's big contribution to the strategy debate is around competition. Key ideas are his five forces of competition and his idea of generic strategies. The latter argues that there are only three general strategies for doing better – you can be the cost leader in efficiency, you can differentiate yourself through unique offerings, or you can focus on niche markets. Simple.

2. **Igor Ansoff:** perhaps the man with the most exotic name among management gurus. He valued detailed planning *within*

frameworks. He is, perhaps, most famous for his eponymous matrix, arguing that all business development can be reduced to four key strategies around offerings (products) – existing and new – or customers – existing and new. (See **Step 7**.) These strategies represent important areas for focus.

3. **Henry Mintzberg:** almost the exact opposite of Ansoff. He believes that strategy is a case of being crafted and developed along the way, rather than something rationally thought through to the end and then rolled out in its finished form. Mintzberg's big thought is the idea of *emergent strategy* – you should keep watching for what works and incorporate that into your strategic work. (He also believes that many CEOs spend significant time pretending that the strategy worked when, in fact, it did not.)

4. **Michael Hammer:** worked alongside his colleague James Champy on the key idea of business process design and business process improvement. This promised significant improvement by reshaping the way processes are delivered through business process reengineering. This has been shown to fail at the mega level and is now more often used to try to improve processes in teams.

5. **Kaplan and Norton:** came up with the balanced scorecard – the idea that businesses were obsessed with financial results when people, customers and internal processes were all part of the integrated web. This has since moved on from the scorecard, which measures results, towards the strategy map – see **Step 9** – which works by following the how/why of any strategic plan.

6. **Kim and Mauborgne:** developed one of the really big ideas of the 1990s – red ocean/blue ocean (see **Skill 9**). Red ocean is the world of things which are defined and accepted and where competition is very close and very tight – for example, supermarket chains in the UK. In blue ocean there is a significant differentiator – a completely new kind of customer or offering. Cirque du Soleil, the Canadian theatre company, completely changed the circus paradigm by removing the animals, aiming it at adults, giving the show a narrative and massively upscaling the event. This is a powerful example of the pursuit of blue ocean advantage.

7. **John Kotter:** an unusual strategy guru in the sense that his big space is in change. We would argue that any strategy involves change. What is interesting about Kotter is that he looks at the change process by itself and he has come up with eight different stages – establish a sense of urgency, create a guiding coalition, develop a clear shared vision, make it a vision, empower people to act, create short-term wins, consolidate gains and make the change stick. It is important to understand Kotter's approach if you are having a problem getting support for your strategic idea.

8. **Jim Collins:** the inventor of the Good to Great model. This offers a framework for transformational change in results through three key disciplines – disciplined people, disciplined thought and disciplined action. Each of these disciplines divides up into two further disciplines with catchy names like 'get the right people on the bus', 'confront the brutal facts' and 'the hedgehog concept'. Collins' definition of *greatness* is a level of financial performance seven times greater than the stock market average over an extended period of time. There may be other measures. It is also worth looking at Collins' subsequent books – e.g. *How the Mighty Fall* – where he reviews his initial thinking.

9. **Kjell Nordström and Jonas Ridderstråle:** two of very few Europeans on this list. Their most influential book is *Funky Business,* which focuses on the talent management and leadership side of strategy. Here is their big idea in summary: 'Traditional roles, jobs, skills, ways of doing things, insights, strategies, aspirations, fears and expectations no longer count. In this environment we cannot have business as usual. We need *business as unusual.* We need different business. We need innovative business. We need unpredictable business. We need surprising business. We need funky business.'

10. **Rosabeth Moss Kanter:** sadly, one of the few women and genuine gurus in the world of management consultancy and management academics. Her big focus has been on change, especially how large organisations manage to change. One of her most influential books is *The Change Masters,* about how companies succeed by developing open communications systems and decentralising resources. She was also an early

advocate – in *When Giants Learn to Dance* – of non-hierarchical structures, which focus on shaping processes rather than observing rules.

11. **Rita McGrath:** an expert on strategy in uncertain, volatile environments. The guru heir to Mintzberg, McGrath's key big idea is discovery-driven planning. In conventional planning, the effectiveness of a plan is judged by how close the outcome comes to the stated projections. But in discovery-driven planning, there are key points when those outcomes are challenged and reviewed. So it is a more iterative approach. Her most recent book *The End of Competitive Advantage: How to Keep Your Strategy Moving as Fast as Your Business* (2013) could be seen as a critique of Michael Porter.

Your list starts here

So, some top gurus but, as in fashion, the list *starts* here, it does not *stop* here. Keep reading *Harvard Business Review* and *Fast Company* to find out what is next or who is next.

Part 3

10 strategy challenges in action

Challenge 1   Post mortem: how to learn when a strategy goes wrong

Challenge 2   #me: how to develop powerful personal branding

Challenge 3   Think fast and slow: how to make difficult choices

Challenge 4   Pivot: how to change the plan on the move

Challenge 5   Look and learn: how to work with consultants

Challenge 6   Smarter strategy: how to develop double loop learning

Challenge 7   Careful! How to manage organisational risk

Challenge 8   Mind your back: how to manage personal risk

Challenge 9   Only 24 hours: how to balance short- and long-term priorities

Challenge 10   Napkin-based strategy: how to explain your idea informally

Post mortem: how to learn when a strategy goes wrong

One of the key messages in this book is the idea that strategy rarely turns out as you expect. Agility – the ability to change direction or pivot – is key. (For more on this, see **Challenge 4**.) However, sometimes it is clear that the strategy has gone quite catastrophically wrong and you need some tools or approaches to:

- analyse what went wrong and how to avoid repeating it
- identify what, if anything, can be fixed to allow you to continue.

Tips to help you learn when a strategy goes wrong

Do not shoot the messenger . . . or anyone else

Approach your initial analysis of why a project or strategy went wrong as a post mortem, *not* as a trial. If you set out to judge and begin by allocating blame, the one thing you know is that everyone will point the finger at someone else. There will not be a queue to accept responsibility.

A post mortem, on the other hand, is about discovering the facts, the data, the information (see white-hat thinking in **Step 8**) and not about attributing blame or responsibility.

A good framework for a post-mortem approach is the model first used by the US Army and, subsequently, by the International Red Cross. Both organisations conduct an *after action review* following every activity, whether or not it has been successful. At this review there are only three questions on the table:

1. **What happened?** A question designed to discover what precise activities took place, in what sequence and what the outputs were.

2. **What was supposed to happen?** A question designed to enable reflection on what the original plan was and what the original concerns or activities were.

3. **Why was there a difference?** A question designed to compare the two sets of data collected in Q1 and Q2 and to establish why there was a gap between the two.

Make these questions the agenda for your next post mortem and see just how constructive this approach to analysis can be.

Focus on what has worked

A second option is to use appreciative inquiry (AI). In this methodology, you do not even consider what went wrong, but focus and build on only the things that worked.

AI is an interesting approach and builds a lot on the positive psychology approach. Of course, the reality is, if the project overall was a disaster and you are sitting surrounded by thousands of packets of freeze-dried bananas that no one wants and the only thing you know is that you learned how to successfully freeze dry them, then AI might not be enough. But it *is* an interesting approach.

 You can find out more about it on this video:

www.thebusinessgym.net

Separate cause from effect

Ishikawa (aka fishbone) analysis is a way of identifying and separating the cause and effect aspects of any problem. This can help you either to establish the strategy you want to take or to assess why a strategy did not work.

It uses a visual image – shaped like a fish – to work back from a specific problem or negative consequences to a number of different areas to check for causes or effects. The tool was developed by Kaoru Ishikawa, a Japanese management consultant and quality guru, in the late 1970s. It was used originally in the car industry and then expanded to other industries.

Central to Ishikawa is the notion of cause and effect – showing how they are linked but distinct. The underlying premise is that, if we get locked into effects, we may not address real causes or we may address only the easiest one or the most obvious.

So the statement 'We don't have enough theatre goers coming to the shows' could lead you to say, 'Let's spend more on advertising and marketing.' But the reality is that the reason more people do not come is because of the kind of shows – or the fact the theatre is too cold, etc. You need to explore *all* possible causes and then identify the key one. (So, it could be that the reason so few people are coming is because the recession has made it too pricey to attend the theatre.)

Of course, a problem may have a number of causes and effects and the following diagram provides a way to check these out around a number of factors. We have developed eight factors, based around the letter P. These are illustrated in the diagram.

Ishikawa is easiest done in a group. You will need an initial challenge or problem definition and, ideally, 3–8 people to help tackle the challenge. It is easiest to do with flipchart paper and felt pens in a workshop setting.

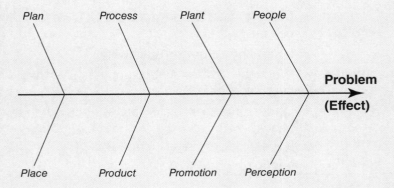

Let us use an under-performing customer helpline as an example. You begin by writing down what you understand to be the problem or effect on the far right. State it as concretely as you can, e.g. '20 per cent of calls to the customer helpline are unsuccessful'.

Then work through the 8Ps checklist to identify any possible causes of the negative consequence, using these stimulus questions:

P issue	Stimulus questions
People	• Do we have the right people doing the work? • Are there enough of them? • Are they trained appropriately?
Place	• Is the location suitable for staff to deliver the service? • Is it in the best place for customers? • Does it make cost sense to have the service there?
Process	• Is the process efficient? • Do staff/customers understand the process? • Is there a more efficient process we can adopt?
Plant	• Do we have the right kit to deliver the service? • Do we need more kit to deal with demand? • Do staff/volunteers understand the kit?
Product	• Is this the right service/product for the audience? • Do customers need a different offering for new needs? • Is demand saturated or slowing?
Promotion	• Is this the right marketing approach for the customers? • Do customers need a different product for new needs? • Is demand saturated so that there is a new need?

P issue	Stimulus questions
Plan	• Did we anticipate demand accurately?
	• Was the planning process itself good?
	• Is there a need to revise the plan radically?
Perception	• Do stakeholders perceive the purpose accurately?
	• Is there confusion on who for?
	• Is there confusion on what is it for?

Once you have listed all the possible causes, add them as horizontal lines under each of the Ps on the fishbone – see the diagram below. You then need to prioritise them: A = high impact; B = medium impact; C = low impact.

The customer helpline fails to deal effectively with one in four calls. (The problem is on the right.) In a workshop, you and the team have come up with a number of reasons for this failure – written on the horizontal lines under the relevant P – and ABC'ed them. The priority now is to deal with the As. So, you draw up an action plan that addresses the A issues: 'train staff better in speedy call handling' if it is 'time they take to handle calls' that is the major problem. Or 'upgrade the system' to tackle the plant challenge.

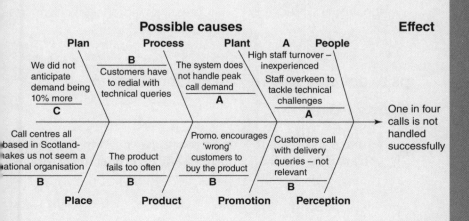

167

#me: how to develop powerful personal branding

Often, it can feel like the challenge to your strategy is not about your thinking, but about you. Unfortunately, the reality is that, if you are young, a woman, a junior in the hierarchy, very introverted, or even of a different ethnicity or culture from the rest of your colleagues, you may experience discrimination that is nothing to do with the quality of your ideas. To deal with this, think about developing a personal brand that helps to build or reinforce your persona as a strategic thinker.

What is personal branding?

Personal branding is 'the process whereby people and their careers are marketed as brands'. The concept suggests that success can come partly from self-packaging and promotion – creating or re-creating yourself as an asset with a definable and desirable value. Aspects of personal brand can relate to personality, knowledge or brains, dress, appearance, motivations and, even, physique.

Tips to develop a powerful personal brand

Clarify the real you

 To make the most of your presence, you need to decide who you are now and then who you want to be or come across as.

Begin by creating an accurate analysis of who you are – a personal SWOT, similar to the company SWOT you did in **Step 3**. Here are questions to stimulate your thinking:

Personal SWOT analysis

	+	−
Internal	• What am I good at? What talents, knowledge, skill do I have relevant to my change role? • What experience or background do I have that will help me in the future change? • What previous experience of change do I have that is or might be useful?	• What am I less good at – talents, knowledge, skill that may be missing and important in my work? • What experience or background do I not have that may hinder me in my change work? • What kinds of change project am I nervous about or reluctant to tackle – and why?
External	• What positive challenges are coming up that might help me in my career and role? • What development opportunities/ interesting projects could I take advantage of to develop? • Who – individuals or agencies, internal or external – could help me in my development and role?	• What challenges are there – competition, role, perceptions – that might cause problems? • What personal or professional risks does/ might my role or task involve me in? • Are there any discriminations I need to challenge – or anyone who does not value my interests?

From this analysis, identify:

- the most significant strengths you can build on
- the most challenging weaknesses you need to address
- the most important opportunities to grasp
- the significant threats to face up to and deal with.

Use these priorities to help you decide who you are and what the possibilities are.

Next, work out what others say about you. Get friends or colleagues to check out your self-perception. Is it accurate?

The ABC of branding

When looking at your personal brand, also consider your A, B, C:

Ambition: What is your mission or ambition? Where do you see your career going? How do you want to add value?	
Beliefs: What are your guiding beliefs or principles? What informs your action and approach? Why do you do what you do?	
Competencies: What are you good at? What skills, abilities and knowledge do you have – and what do you think you will need in the future?	

Define your USPs in your ABCs!

Within your ABC you need to include some USPs. USP stands for unique selling proposition – the quality that makes someone or something stand out from other similar options. So, a VW car has more or less the same specification as any other car at the similar price point. But a VW's USP – the distinguishing dimension – is about safety.

Many – or at least a number of – other people have similar qualifications, ability and experience to you. The question, then, is how to stand out. You can do this by thinking about what is distinctive and unusual about you that makes you different. What else do you bring to the party in terms of beliefs and values, skills, experience, ability or knowledge? Go back to the ABC and make sure there is something distinctive listed.

Learn from other brands

Think about a present or past colleague whom you admire and whom you have seen being successful at developing or selling strategy/ideas:

- What qualities or values does this person have? How are these important in underpinning their personal brand?

- How does this person portray these qualities through actions – in meetings, presentations, in one to ones?
- What can you learn from this analysis or observation? How can you apply the learning?

Revisit your ABC again and see if there is anything you can add.

Define your brand

OK, let us define your brand in terms of a number of elements. Some of these are listed below. It is not exhaustive, but we have included:

- intellect and competencies
- personality and outlook
- dress and appearance
- values and beliefs.

Add more elements of your own.

Under each element, you then need to explore the relevant aspect or dimension. For example, under intellect and competencies, you could have 'knowledgeable about marketing' and 'well read'. The last column – how you *do* or *will* convey it – needs to include specific behaviours or actions, such as 'speak more loudly in meetings' or 'dress in a more formal business way at work'.

Brand elements	Aspects/dimensions	How will I convey it?
Intellect and competencies	Appearing knowledgeable about various strategy theories	Make sure I read *Harvard Business Review* every month and can mention key gurus

Anticipate the challenging messages

Some of the audience/interviewers may have negative concerns about you, based on personal knowledge of you or arising from your CV. List the three main concerns you think you can anticipate – e.g.

'she's soft on xyz. . . ' – and how you might answer the criticism, if asked.

Be aware that sometimes concerns are hidden. In an apparently diversity-friendly setting, sexism might still rear its ugly head in an indirect way. For example, 'She's a young woman. Does she have the gravitas to run what has been a male-dominated team?' You need to have an answer ready, whether the concern is implicit or explicit.

To tackle this, make two lists:

- What challenges or questions might I be asked – and what will be thought but not asked?
- What are my responses? How can I make sure that I have evidence to underpin the response?

Keep it real

It is very tempting, when faced with a challenging question, to gloss over or dismiss your weaknesses. We suggest this is *not* a good idea. Instead, we encourage you to keep it real – and, even, perhaps disclose some appropriate weaknesses or shortcomings.

There is quite a lot of scientific data that suggests that being candid and balanced about your weaknesses adds to credibility. The classic study was run in the 1970s by psychologists Edward Jones and Eric Gordon from Duke University. The experiment involved a researcher being recorded talking about his life from a script. Two groups of volunteers were asked to listen to different versions. In one he admitted that he had been expelled from school for cheating, but went on to explain that he had seen the error of his ways. In another, he simply reported his career without mentioning the expulsion.

Interestingly, the results for this experiment and several further iterations have remained consistent. When the researcher admitted the expulsion, it made him more likeable to the volunteers. The implication is we like people to be fallible. These results have been replicated elsewhere in different situations. For example, a lawyer mentioning the weakness in their case in court and then dealing with it, rather than trying to brush it under the carpet.

We like people and organisations to be honest with us. What weaknesses/failings might you share with your colleagues? And how could you share them so they add to your credibility rather than reduce it?

Sum it up

OK, now you need to sum up your personal brand. Write a new 100-word biography as though it was for LinkedIn or the top of your CV. If you are embarrassed about saying positive things about yourself, write in the third person, 'Chris is an ambitious, clear thinking. . . '.

 If you need ideas, tips or hints on personal branding, go to: www.thebusinessgym.net

Think fast and slow: how to make difficult choices

All strategy is about choices but, sometimes, it is not clear how to select the best option:

- If there are competing stakeholders, it may not be possible to reconcile their different interests.
- Two options may be so different that it is difficult to compare – so oranges and bananas are both nice fruits but are hard to compare directly.
- One of the options may appear attractive and popular and one may be unpopular and tough – the temptation is to go with the popular one.
- An option may have a long cycle time – that is, the success may not be clearly established until some way down the line.

So, probably, you need something more sophisticated than tossing a coin.

Tips to help make a choice

Clarify what is important and to whom

There are times when the best way to decide your strategy is to make an impact and importance matrix. This looks at a number of key success factors (KSFs) for any strategy and then matches them against the interests of key stakeholders. The number in the box where KSFs and stakeholders meet then represents the strength of opinion on a scale from 1–5, with 1 being relatively unimportant and 5 being very important.

Looking at the following matrix example you can see that:

- the key success factor for all stakeholders is for a speedy solution
- stakeholders are divided about cost
- a key stakeholder – the CEO – has a particular opinion on the cost issue
- no one really cares about the location issue – so it is not a KSF.

Key success factors (KSFs)

	Move the A&E function to another hospital	Save money	Reduce staff stress	Reduce patient wait	Improve hospital 'rank'	Deliver bonuses	Create positive PR
Stakeholders	CEO	9	5	7	9	1	9
	Doctors	3	9	7	9	6	5
	Nurses	3	9	7	5	9	5
	Patients	1	1	9	1	1	5
	Ambulance drivers	1	−5	5	1	1	1
	KSF score	17	19	35	25	18	25

Whatever solution or strategy you adopt, it should meet as many stakeholders' needs as possible. You can then use this matrix as both a scorecard and a communications framework as the strategy develops:

- It is a scorecard in that you can establish whether you have delivered a particular KSF to a particular stakeholder.
- It is a communications framework that will make sure you let key stakeholders know which of their interests have been met and which have not.

Decide on data… watch for feelings

Daniel Kahneman won the Nobel Prize for economic sciences in 2002. Ironically, he has never taken a course in economics – he is a psychologist. He wrote an enormously influential book you should read called *Thinking, Fast and Slow*.

One part of his thesis is that we often make decisions based on irrational feelings or ill-informed opinions – called heuristics – rather than on data – facts and figures. At the same time, we think we are making rational judgements about the house we buy, the investments we make or even the products we choose. The two systems we use to make choices are:

- **System 1:** operates automatically and quickly, with little or no effort and no sense of voluntary control, like the autopilot in a plane.

- **System 2:** allocates attention to the mental activities that demand effort, including deciding complex issues, like the actual pilot in the plane.

As far as possible, you should try to base your decisions on data and make sure you have the most robust data you can to justify your decisions. To test how good you are at system 1 and system 2, try this quiz:

System 1 and 2 quiz

Q1   Choose between definitely getting £900 or a 90 per cent chance of getting £1,000. Which would you prefer?

   A   Getting £900

   B   90 per cent chance of getting £1,000

Q2   Choose between definitely losing £900 or a 90 per cent chance of losing £1,000. Which would you prefer?

   A   Losing £900

   B   90 per cent chance of losing £1,000

(See the end of the chapter for what your choices say about your preference.)

10:10:10

Another great and simple way to decide your strategy is to zoom in and then zoom out, using the 10:10:10 formula. This asks you to consider the long- and short-term implications of your choice.

Ask yourself the following questions:

- If I decide to adopt this strategy, what will the implications be in *10 minutes*? (Will I be uncertain again? Will some key people be shaken or angry? Will others be excited?)

- If I decide to adopt this strategy, what will the implications be in *10 months*? (Will we know if the strategy has been successful by then? Will I need to have a Plan B, if it has not worked? Will we need a next phase?)
- If I decide to adopt this strategy, what will the implications be in *10 years*? (Will the strategy be out of date by then? Will I need to have relaunched it? Will I still be here? Will this be a career-maker for me?)

These three questions allow you to zoom in on the short-term implications and zoom out on the long-term ones.

System 1 and 2 answer

Most participants answer A and then B to this two-part question. Kahneman and his colleague Amos Tversky used this question and others to illustrate what is now called prospect theory, an aspect of system 1 and 2. They claim the AB answer illustrates a specific behavioural tendency – when people face a gain, they become risk averse; when they face a loss, they become risk seeking. This quite revolutionary general principle severely challenges utility theory, a cornerstone of rational economic thought since the 18th century.

Pivot: how to change the plan on the move

What is a pivot?

One of the key ideas in contemporary management thinking is the pivot – refocusing a business or a significant aspect of what your business does to find a higher performing model. Pivots most often come from an awareness that the current approach does not work. And, although normally associated with start-ups, increasingly mature organisations are considering how to pivot.

Two examples of pivoting organisations at either end of the maturity spectrum are Groupon and IBM. Groupon, the deals site, even now probably blocking your inbox with junk mail offers, famously pivoted from its original mission, which was to organise social advocacy campaigns in the style of Avaaz. But Groupon could not make the cyber activism model work and turned, instead, into a billion-dollar daily deal site. IBM saw the writing on the wall for hardware production after many decades and pivoted to become a management consultancy, in the process selling its hardware business to Lenovo.

A number of charities have also made successful pivots. Macmillan Cancer Support pivoted from 'end of life palliative care' to a broader 'living with cancer' proposition, as it recognised many cancers were becoming chronic rather than a death sentence. And Lepra, which used to be focused on leprosy, successfully used its competence in dealing with infectious diseases to pivot into tackling TB and other similar illnesses.

Sometimes, a pivot is described as simply changing the customer product or service offering. And many pivots do turn on these two options. But, in fact, it can involve a change in a number of different elements in your business model. In practice, a pivot can involve a change in customers, product or offering, the revenue model or pricing, the cost structure, acquisition channels, distribution channels, resources used, core activities and, even, partners.

 Choosing the right area on which to pivot is key.

Pivoting is not easy. Eric Ries, who came up with the Lean Startup methodology, and who can claim to have popularised the term *pivot*, is clear that he means keeping one foot firmly in place as you shift the other in a new direction.

With this in mind, it is essential that organisations build on what they have learned from past success – and analyse failure accurately. When you have done this, you can then apply these insights to refocus for success. One key to the 'one foot firm' approach is to make sure you play to your core competencies. Begin by asking 'What are we outstandingly good at?' only when you have identified that can you begin to consider which of the other eight business model options you can pivot on.

Pivot power

As ever, the real insights often come from practical examples. Here are two famous pivots – one old and one new.

1. Wrigley's chewing gum

Pivoting is not a new idea. One of the earliest examples comes from the famous Wrigley's chewing gum in the early 20th century. The founder, William Wrigley, stumbled on the idea of a chewing gum business while giving it away. In the 1890s he had a job selling domestic products, such as soap and baking powder door-to-door. To improve sales, he developed the idea of offering free chewing gum with every sale. He noticed the chewing gum was more popular than his real products. So, he pivoted and went on to make his own chewing gum. Today, the company grosses billions of dollars and is an iconic US brand.

2. Twitter

One of the most famous pivots in recent years has been the way in which Odeo pivoted into the altogether more famous Twitter. So, Odeo – which you have never heard of – began life as an online network that allowed people to subscribe to podcasts. It was doing reasonably well, but then Apple began to dominate the podcast space through iTunes. It looked like curtains for Odeo. But they decided to ask all employees to try to come up with a new business proposition. The additional challenge was that it had to happen in two weeks, before they ran out of money. Two employees had the bizarre idea of microblogging. The founders decided to give it a try. The rest is history.

Tips to help change tack and pivot

- **Let go of the past:** a pivot will involve you letting go of time and energy – and maybe even money – that you have invested. But, to move on, you need to be prepared to let go of the past.
- **Understand your business' strengths and weaknesses:** you should have no problem listing the things your company or team does well, and those you do poorly. This analysis will help you build on what works.
- **Seek internal insights:** encourage everyone in your team or company to contribute ideas and insights that might allow you to change. (See the Twitter example above.) Good ideas can come from anywhere – be open to them!
- **Identify pivot options:** once you have got some insights, narrow them down to three or four key options that you might pursue. By all means, collect data on these options – but do not spend too long – pivots tend to happen fast.
- **Evaluate the opportunity:** when you have established an opportunity, think about how to roll it out. Do not be afraid to prototype – to try things out. Pivoting hardly ever works perfectly the first time. Try it and then improve it.
- **Sell the pivot to your team:** successful pivots need the support of your team, early adopters, customers and, perhaps, even investors. Explain why you are doing what you are doing – and seek feedback. Above all, sell it to your customers.

- **Just do it:** you need a plan to pivot and you need to put it into action – combining team, tasks and time. Ensure that everyone is aware of his or her role in the pivot, how it impacts on them and how critical their contribution is.
- **Stay lean and agile:** remember that pivoting may happen several times. You may need to evaluate emerging threats and seize new opportunities. You must be willing to disrupt your own business model over and over again.

Darwin was – and still is – often misquoted, which caused him considerable irritation. He never talked about 'survival of the fittest'. In fact, what he said was:

'It is not the strongest of the species that survives, nor the most intelligent, but the one most responsive to change.'

Charles Darwin, *The Origin of Species*

Sounds like a pivot manifesto!

Look and learn: how to work with consultants

At some point in your career, you will work with or use external consultants for strategy development. Consultants are big in strategy!

Who are consultants and what do they do?

Consultants are individuals – who either work for a company or are self-employed – hired to provide expertise or advice to a team or, even, whole organisation. For example, Pope Francis hired McKinsey Consultants to advise on the restructuring of the Catholic Church. They worked with him to develop some critical changes in an organisation that had been doing badly for some time and, as a result, Pope Francis:

- **set leadership style:** he got rid of the expensive trappings of the role, such as Gucci shoes, and drove around in an old car
- **focused on core business:** he made it clear that the core issues that the Church would deal with were to do with social justice not abstract theology
- **restructured the management:** he cleared out a number of incompetent senior cardinals – and those involved in scandals
- **repositioned the brand:** famously, he repositioned the Church as 'on the side of the poor' – having taken on the brand name of Francis.

There are significant advantages to using consultants. They can:

- be very cost-effective when you need specific expertise in a specific area for a specific period of time on a specific project

- provide additional capacity, if your team is overstretched or if you are trying to take on a new project that otherwise would not be delivered
- offer a level of objectivity – or even be able to see or articulate challenges others either cannot see or fail to comment on.

Of course, there may also be downsides. They can:

- impose solutions that are inappropriate – attractive on paper but impractical in reality
- undermine your credibility by suggesting that you do not really know enough about your own work or expertise
- pick your brains, package your ideas as their own and subtly sell them back to senior management at a premium.

Tips to work effectively with consultants

Clarify there is a need

Often, the temptation is to reach for the telephone and call in external expertise when, in fact, the skills or knowledge you need exist somewhere else in your team, department or company. Job one probably is to ensure that you do not already have the expertise internally. It will, almost certainly, be cheaper and may well be more targeted than you can find externally.

Establish how they will tackle the job

Having read this book, probably you will have a good idea of the range of techniques and frameworks a consultant might use to develop a strategy. Do not be afraid to ask them why they would choose a particular model. And take whatever opportunities you can to learn from them how to use the techniques in action – or any alternatives they might use. It is your chance to improve your understanding.

Make sure you have sanction to do it

If it is your decision to use management consultants, make sure that you follow an appropriate procedure. This could involve having the brief or terms of reference signed off by senior managers. It may also involve following a procurement policy – perhaps getting three quotations or working within a fee limit. Consultants – like builders – can be expensive. Their priority is often to maximise their income – based on the number of hours spent on an activity. Make sure you secure from them a clear scale of fees against outputs. Do not sign up to an open-ended commitment.

Secure a written outline on the steps the consultant will take, how long these steps will take and the costs involved. Most consultants are comfortable with providing written proposals and accounting for their time on a weekly or monthly basis.

Make sure everyone knows about the arrangements

Consultants may not be threatening to you, but they can appear threatening to other people. So, make sure that everyone knows you have hired one and what exactly they will do. (And will not do.) If you yourself have not been told what the consultant is meant to do, do not be afraid to ask. In this case, knowledge and understanding really help to integrate everyone in the action.

Ensure you get regular reports

The nature of a consultancy assignment often will change as it progresses. A regular report allows you to know whether the project is on track or whether some really urgent renegotiation needs to take place. Make sure you get your reports, or even just an update, at less formal, but still regular, meetings.

Review the effectiveness of the consultancy intervention when it is done

As we said before, a consultant is an expensive investment. After an assignment is finished, you should undertake a review of how effective they were, how well you used them and what you gained. The after action review framework in **Challenge 1** is a good way to do this.

Smarter strategy: how to develop double loop learning

Sometimes, a strategy does not work, despite the fact you try to refine and improve it. You seem to be locked in a Sisyphean cycle of working harder and harder but still not making real progress.

This can lead to frustration and failure for you, the team and, in the long term, the company. When you spot that more effort is not leading to results you want, you may need to learn strategically or at a more fundamental level. This is sometimes characterised as the move from what is called single loop to double loop learning.

Double loop learning was identified and codified by two US academics, Argyris and Schön, in the 1970s. It has since become an enormously influential model or framework for organisational learning overall.

Argyris and Schön argue that individuals, and even groups, have mental models that tend to reinforce whatever their current approach is. 'If only we improved the way we do telemarketing – made the product more sexy – then things would get better.' Sometimes, you need to challenge these models and look behind the built-in assumptions. Again, as a relatively junior member of staff, you can spot these challenges more readily.

This kind of fundamental rethinking links strongly to the red ocean/blue ocean approach we discussed in **Skill 9**. If you remember, Cirque du Soleil succeeded partly by breaking the mental model of what a circus should be – and then improving on their radical new model.

Let us distinguish specifically between the two learning loops – illustrated in the diagram below:

- **Double loop learning** encourages you to look more deeply into the cause of any challenge *and* the action. Any feedback is used to review the whole process right back to the governing variables – exploring the fundamental principles and ideas, even the business models, underpinning your strategy. So, considering what a circus should be is part of a double loop approach.

- **Single loop learning** aims to solve any specific problems that arise from implementation only by making changes in the action. The focus is on becoming more efficient or effective – getting better at doing. There is no attempt to go back to first principles. If Cirque du Soleil had stuck with single loop learning, they would have focused on more and better acts, more exotic animals, etc.

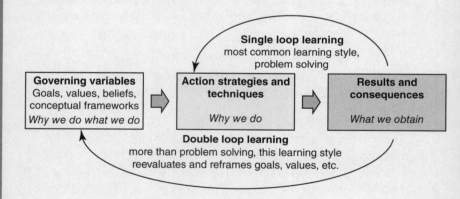

For a simple personal example, take losing weight. In single loop learning, if your diet is not reaping the desired result, you might look to sticking to it more strictly if you have been cheating every now and then or trying a different diet. In double loop learning, you would go right back to look at your motivation for losing weight. This might lead you to take more exercise or even to consider whether you really need to lose weight. Are you just responding to social pressure to be thin?

Tips to move from single to double loop learning

Keep an eye on the changing world

You are, no doubt, aware of the challenges faced by a number of UK supermarkets at the time of writing – 2015 – especially Morrisons and Tesco.

Both chains worked very hard at developing their existing successful models and building them at scale – single loop learning. But, as they did this, they failed to notice that customer priorities had changed, the way people shopped had altered, and they failed to notice what successful low-budget rivals were doing. (That would have been double loop learning.) So, Morrisons concentrated on expanding its existing successful model – but missed the online delivery business and the growth in smaller, convenience-style stores.

Tesco also had a problem. It thought customers wanted choice and that is where it focused its efforts – to the point that, in January 2015, it had 224 kinds of air freshener, 283 kinds of coffee and 28 kinds of ketchup on the shelves. (In contrast, low-cost rival Aldi has one kind of ketchup in one size, a mere 12 kinds of air freshener and only 20 kinds of coffee.) Tesco has since announced it is cutting the range of lines it has by 30 per cent, as part of a programme to fundamentally change the way it does business. Some double loop learning at last – but very late.

Are you keeping an eye on what other companies and your customers are doing? Or assuming they will respond to improvements in your process?

Loop fast

We need to learn to loop faster as business cycle times become shorter and more volatile. In businesses such as mobile phones, pop music or the fashion industry, it is essential they can try out new things quickly and learn what works and what does not equally speedily.

Take the fashion chain Zara. It famously changed its business model to be fast. It stopped trying to predict what would be hot by attending fashion shows and producing high street versions of the catwalk. Now it sees itself as being in the logistics business. It puts a range of styles in its shops, monitors what sells – and makes more of it. Zara can restock any shop in under five days – in a sense it has created a double loop where you let it know what is fashionable and it pays attention and adapts. It learned what business it was in and created a model to dictate what it should make.

How fast do you need to be in your business? Do you need to get faster to keep up with changes?

Ask 'Why?' five times

A famous Zen approach to take you back to first principles is to ask 'Why?' five times. Begin with 'Why are we doing *this* specific action?' and then work back. This will expose what you or colleagues think are the underlying principles behind any strategy.

Reflect more

There is a terrible pressure in business to be seen to be *doing* all the time. Double loop learning encourages you to reflect more.

 Spending time thinking not just about *what* works, but about *why* it works, can be revealing.

Einstein used to conduct what he called thought experiments by lying on the grass outside his Zurich laboratory dreaming about what the principles underlying the universe might be. In this way, he was able to move away from the simplistic Newtonian approach to physics that had dominated for hundreds of years. His dreaming allowed him to imagine some new fundamental principles at work.

Careful! How to manage organisational risk

The fundamental nature of strategy means that it involves risk. You are hoping, not assuming, that if you do X it will lead to Y and then to Z. And the idea is that that is all positive. (For example, improve the brochure X leads to greater customer awareness Y which, in turn, leads to higher sales Z.) That is strategy as a hypothesis. See **Steps 9** and **10** for a further discussion of this idea.

Since it is only a hypothesis you have a responsibility, with your colleagues, to try to ensure that the organisational, department or team risk is reduced and, ideally, minimised. So, if your strategy does not work out, at least impact is manageable.

Famously, of course, a number of organisations have bet heavily on a specific strategic approach and it has gone horrifically wrong. Some examples include:

- The change from Coke to New Coke – though this decision was quickly reversed.
- The Sinclair C5 – a one-person electric vehicle which brought the previously successful Sinclair empire to its knees.
- Blockbuster's decision to stick with stores and avoid streaming internet films – which led to the demise of a market leader.
- Google Glass – which was going to change the way that we interact with wearable technology.

And there are even more catastrophic examples. Lehman Brothers' failure in 2008 signalled the start of the global crash.

The massive oil spill following the explosion on the Deepwater Horizon oil platform in 2010 created environmental havoc in the Gulf of Mexico. In each case, there was weak risk management at a number of levels.

Tips to help manage organisational risk

Create a risk-aware, but not risk-averse, mindset

One of the most effective strategies to reduce or avoid risk is to ensure everyone is aware of potential challenges – and is actively looking out for them. Often, an individual or a team will have a sense of a potential challenge before a machine even registers it. So it is important they feel they can raise concerns about high-risk issues. This open communication mindset needs to be signalled at the highest levels of leadership – and reflected in your own practice if you are a team or department leader.

At the same time, people need to be sensible about risk or nothing new or really creative will ever be tried. Think of the Apollo moon missions or the countless scientists who have used themselves as guinea pigs in the pursuit of an idea that needs to be proved to work. Good risk management does not stop innovation or creativity.

Buy a whistle and do not be afraid to blow it!

Not all potential risks will be in your control or line of sight. But, when they are – and you see something start to go wrong that you cannot deal with and no one else is taking action on – you may need to seriously consider whether you should whistle-blow. Most man-made disasters – including the global crash and Deepwater Horizon – could have been stopped by someone, in quite a modest position, raising the alarm with more senior managers.

 Whatever you do, do not sign up to the not-my-job mentality.

Make distinctions between different types of risk

There are, of course, different types of risk at different levels that need a different response. Here is a broad typology and how you can or might respond:

- **External context risk:** there will always be bad weather, typhoons, earthquakes, etc. And, when these happen, you need to have a risk management strategy in place. For example, there were weak processes in place at Fukushima Daiichi Nuclear Power Plant to handle the aftermath of the Great East Japan earthquake and tsunami in 2011. This was despite the fact that Japan is both heavily dependent on nuclear energy *and* sits on the Pacific Ring of Fire, where 90 per cent of the world's earthquakes occur. Do not be afraid to point out the seemingly obvious external risk that could affect your company.

- **Calculated risks:** some risks involve a strategic decision that may have significant consequences, but these can be worked out – maybe even mathematically – and are manageable. For example, an oil company deciding to buy significant amounts of oil at one price in the hope that it will go up is, clearly, a strategic risk. As, at a simple level, is the decision to order lots of red wine for the staff party you are organising when you do not know what people like to drink! Analysts need to spend time working out how acceptable this level of strategic risk is (or asking a selection of people what their favourite tipple is).

- **Performance or compliance risks:** these are internal risks that should be avoidable with proper processes. So, a performance management system is designed to ensure employees do their jobs properly – and to ensure someone takes timely remedial action where this is not happening. If you are a fan of *The Simpsons'* opening credits, you will know neither Homer Simpson, nor the Springfield Nuclear Power Plant management, would pass this test: at the start of every episode, Homer goes home with radioactive material down his trousers. On a more serious note, in the 2014–15 Ebola epidemic, clearly it was essential that medical staff followed every procedure to the letter to avoid contamination. This is an example of a compliance risk with very serious consequences.

Use the 4Ts methodology

For each type of risk, use the 4Ts methodology to plan how to reduce its potential impact:

- **Terminate:** choose a strategy to eliminate the possibility of anything going wrong. This might involve ensuring multiple backup systems or, at a simpler level, insisting that all employees exactly follow official procedure – in this way either removing risk or reducing it to a negligible level.

- **Tolerate:** calculate how acceptable the risk is. This might involve allowing a system to fail once a year or to permit staff to make some judgements because, even if they get it wrong, it will not be mission-critical.

- **Transfer:** move the risk outside. This is what insurance is for – the insurance company assumes the risk if anything goes wrong, rather than you or your company. Or you can use an external agency to handle one of your processes and they then take some of the liability if anything goes awry.

- **Train:** prepare for the risk and train everyone in what action they need to take if anything goes wrong. This might involve rehearsals and/or publishing explicit procedures. For example, Special Forces will train on a number of eventualities for a specific mission. And, of course, fire drills are a form of risk preparation.

Assess impact and likelihood

To assess risk, you need to establish two different factors and work out the mathematical relationship between them:

1. **Impact:** what would be the result if the risk event came to pass? For example, would it be a short period of downtime for the team? Or would there be significant financial loss? Or is there a possibility of someone being hurt? These different kinds of impacts can be graded 1–5, with 1 being relatively low impact and 5 being very high.

2. **Likelihood:** is this event likely to happen within a given period – a day, a week, a month, a year, a century? Statistical data helps to model frequency. So, some things may happen once every

10 years – such as a blizzard in Kent. Using statistical data, you can work out the likelihood of a risk occurring in a given period. The scale is the same (1–5), with 1 being relatively unlikely and 5 being extremely likely.

Any event scoring 5 × 5 clearly needs a lot of preparation!

Is 99.99 per cent good enough?

A famous example of risk and impact often is quoted about whether a company having a 99.99 per cent safety record is entirely acceptable. Of course! Who would not be proud of such a record?

OK, now think about Heathrow airport. 99.99 per cent of planes landing safely would mean three planes crash landing and killing up to 1,000 people – every month. Clearly, neither an acceptable risk nor an acceptable impact.

Mind your back: how to manage personal risk

One of the key messages in this book is the idea that strategy rarely turns out as you expect. Agility – the ability to change direction or pivot (see **Challenge 4**) – is key at an organisational level. However, sometimes you find yourself in a situation at work when the priority is to make sure that you manage the risk to you and your career.

Tips to manage personal risk

Unlike the tips in other challenges, you need to work through *all* these tips – and in sequence.

1. Begin by clarifying the risky situation

What exactly *is* the risky situation? For example, you are worrying because you have been asked to write a new marketing strategy. But what is really the underlying concern? The potential loss to your reputation or carefully built up personal brand? The potential loss of a bonus to you? The potential loss of a promotion opportunity? You need to be clear.

2. Confront your concerns - what are you afraid of?

Answer these three questions:

1. What specifically am I afraid might happen if I tackle this? (What might happen to me? To others?)

2. What is the very *worst* thing that could happen to me? And how *likely* is it to happen? Maybe use the impact-likelihood calculation described towards the end of **Challenge 7**.

3. What can I do to prevent or reduce the *likelihood* of this worst thing happening? Alternatively, can I do anything to reduce the *impact*?

When you have answered these questions, take a break. At this point, you may decide the very worst thing you are afraid of is both too serious and too likely to happen to be ignored. If so, you need to ask yourself if the action you were planning to take is still worth it. If yes, move on to the next tip. If not, try some of the green-hat techniques from **Step 8** to choose a different approach.

3. Consider the consequences of delay

Concern about the level of risk often can result in you delaying or postponing taking action. This can actually be helpful if you are collecting data or seeking advice to help with your decision. But, if you are simply procrastinating, you need to consider the negative consequences to *you* of putting off taking action. Will the opportunity no longer be available?

Next, you need to consider the negative consequences to others (colleagues, the company, even customers or suppliers). Be as specific as you can.

4. Stress the success – what will be the pay-offs if the risk comes off?

Consider what benefits will kick in if this risk comes off. As with consequences, think about the outcomes for you and for others.

What disadvantages will stop for you and others? Will you at least be able to sleep at night once you have taken the risk?

Take another break. At this point, you may want to review your decision on whether to take this action. Is it still worth it, in your opinion?

5. Make momentum - get some pace behind it

It is time to give yourself some motivation momentum.

- How will you reward yourself along the way for working on this risky project or idea?
- How will you reward yourself when it is all done? This may be something just for you – or you may want to organise a team or family celebration.
- Who else might praise or thank you for success – your manager, your boss, customers, suppliers?

6. Seek support - look for resources and advice

Who else – a mentor, a coach, a colleague, a consultant – can you ask in order to check out your plan and the risks?

And, finally, who else can you involve to make the task easier and more achievable? (See the final section of the book on **business buddies and mentors**.)

Only 24 hours: how to balance short- and long-term priorities

Some strategic issues require long-term commitment over a considerable period. Other issues require immediate, practical action. If the long term is sacrificed for the day-to-day, there can be disastrous consequences. Balancing the two is a key skill you need to acquire if you have not already done so.

Tips to help balance short-term and long-term

Building your pyramid

Big strategic projects are like building a pyramid – it takes a long time and it is, fundamentally, difficult. So, it is tempting to put off starting the pyramid and to focus instead on the small work.

To help you get into and, ultimately, achieve your pyramid goal, you need to:

- break it down into task blocks – each of which individually is manageable
- get some momentum (quick) tasks going – such as set up the spreadsheet
- schedule in enough time to plan the project – try a work breakdown structure
- set a deadline and publish it to others – this will help you to meet it
- ask for help and support from others who can also chase you up.

Stop being addicted to urgency

While the idea of long-term strategy appeals, the reality of much contemporary work is that urgency dominates. Urgency demands attention *now*. It is the ringing phone, the 'Can I just have five minutes?' from a colleague to answer their urgent problem (which runs into half an hour), it is deadlines and crises. The problem with urgency is it can be addictive. And the dangers of being addicted to urgency are:

- **it misleads:** it makes you feel important, 'Everyone needs *my* input and efforts'
- **it clouds your judgement:** it gives the illusion of control and validation, 'I'm doing lots of things, therefore I must be successful'
- **it prioritises quick fixes over long-term success:** it gives you permission to avoid tackling the difficult and strategic, 'I really must start on the strategic project . . . tomorrow when I've finished *this*'.

Balancing urgent and important

Stephen Covey is one of the leading authorities on leadership and managing time. In his book *The 7 Habits of Highly Effective People,* he looks at the relationship between urgent and important activities. Covey says we can choose to spend our time in one of four quadrants. Yes, he too has a matrix.

Reflect on your work style

How have you spent your time over the last month or so? In which quadrant – or quadrants – have you been working predominantly? What does it tell you about your work style?

- **Quadrant 1 (Q1)** activities are those that are both urgent (need dealing with now) and important (help deliver us towards our goals). These are significant activities that need immediate action, such as meeting a print deadline for a leaflet you are producing or dealing with an emergency. They are the activities that bring results in the short to medium term.

	Urgent	Not urgent
Important	**Q1**	**Q2**
Not important	**Q3**	**Q4**

- **Quadrant 3 (Q3)** activities are ones that are urgent but not important. These activities often can masquerade as quadrant 1 activities. They are interruptions, some phone calls or a meeting that has little impact. They can be other people's priorities or activities that are enjoyable because they make you feel important. However, that feeling of importance can be at the cost of effectiveness and, as a result, is deceptive. There is always lots to do in this quadrant, but none of it is strategic.

- **Quadrant 4 (Q4)** activities are neither urgent nor important. They are, very often, pleasant activities like web surfing for research, making coffee for the team or socialising. They are distractions from what you should be concentrating on. They are the time wasters and often are respite activities when you are very busy.

- **Quadrant 2 (Q2)** activities are where truly effective and strategic people spend their time. This is where activities are important and not urgent. This is the quadrant where strategic planning is done, where key relationships are built. These activities are where you take time to service the machine rather than keep it running. These are the activities that bring quality and add significant value.

The two types of importance

Covey talks about two types of activity through the fable of the goose and the golden eggs:

'One day a farmer discovered that his goose had laid a golden egg among the ordinary ones. The next day, when collecting the eggs, he noticed she had done the same. Each day the goose laid yet another egg and the farmer grew rich.

But despite amassing great wealth the farmer became greedy for more eggs and so killed the goose to get the eggs all at once. Sadly he discovered no more eggs.'

Clearly, the golden eggs (the results) are important but, if we fail to recognise the importance of taking care of the goose (the capacity to produce the results), we could end up with no eggs (results).

Covey is defining golden eggs (results) as Q1 activities and looking after the goose (capacity to produce results) as Q2.

If you do not focus on Q2...

Let us look at the consequences of spending too much time in Qs 1, 3 and 4.

People who constantly undertake urgent and important activities (Q1) are stressed and feel that they are continuously firefighting. While they deliver results in the short term, they do not have the vision, perspective and successful relationships to sustain long-term strategic success. Too many activities in Q1 leads to crisis management and burnout.

People who are spending a lot of time dealing with urgent but not important activities (Q3) can deceive themselves into thinking they are working in Q1. They chop and change as they react to different situations arising. But they cannot do it all and this leads to broken promises. Ironically, often they can feel victimised and out of control.

People who spend a significant amount of their time doing activities that are not important go from responding to urgent but not important stimuli to trivial time-wasting activities (Q4). They totally lack responsibility and have no impact. They can be exploitative within relationships and can be highly dependent on others or the organisation to meet their needs.

People who invest enough time in activities that are important but not urgent (Q2) are highly successful *and* effective managers. They have vision and perspective and understand the balance between short-term delivery and long-term capacity-building activities. As a result, they deliver *and* have few crises. They are well respected and have strong successful relationships with colleagues.

Become a Q2 manager

Increasing demands at work today push you more and more towards the urgent – the genuine crisis or interruptions. The risk to organisational and personal development is that you lose the ability to balance longer-term need, the sense of perspective and purpose, which is core to a fulfilled work life and organisation success. The quick fix may deliver short-term results but not a sustainable future.

To become genuinely strategic you need to become a quadrant 2 manager.

Napkin-based strategy: how to explain your idea informally

The world grows more complicated every day. Partly, this is because of the sheer volume of data and information we have. Consider the following slightly frightening statistics:

- Bain & Company says nobody really knows how much data there is because the volume is growing so fast. But its estimate is that about 90 per cent of all the data in the world today has been created in the past few years.

- The US Government says that, in 2011, 1.8 zettabytes (or 1.8 trillion gigabytes) of data was created, the equivalent to every US citizen writing three tweets per minute for 26,976 years.

- And it did not get much better in 2012. According to computer giant IBM, 2.5 exabytes – that's 2.5 billion gigabytes – of data was generated every day in 2012. Think how big your laptop hard disc is.

- Finally, an International Data Corporation study predicts data will grow 50 times by 2020, driven not by email or even pictures of cats on Facebook, but largely by systems like sensors in clothing, medical devices, etc.

We are drowning in data. And you probably need to accept that your strategic plan – with its beautiful spreadsheets, graphs and flowcharts – is simply one element in this data deluge. Which means part of your job has to be to cut through the surfeit of data to make your ideas stand out. To do this with whatever ideas you are trying to share, not just your strategic plan, you need to express them simply – or as simply as possible.

How do you do that?

Tips to help keep it simple

KISS

KISS is an acronym for a design principle originally coined by engineer Kelly Johnson, who worked at the Lockheed Corporation on highly sophisticated planes, such as the SR71 Blackbird spy plane. There are disagreements about exactly what he meant it to stand for – the options ranging from the classic 'Keep it simple, stupid!' to 'Keep it short and simple' or, even, 'Keep it simple and straightforward'.

Whatever Johnson meant, he made it clear he meant simplicity should be a key goal in any design and that unnecessary complexity should be avoided. Apparently, this principle was so important to him that he famously handed his team of design engineers a box of tools before giving them a brief. His challenge to them was that the sophisticated aircraft they were designing must be repairable by an average mechanic in the field, under combat conditions, with only the tools in the box. That is true simplicity!

So, no matter how clever your overall concept is, use any of the tools in this book to make sure it is easily understandable. You really do not need any others. This is your strategy toolbox.

Simplicity is not just a modern idea

William of Ockham (c. 1287–1347), the English Franciscan friar, philosopher and theologian, famously coined the phrase 'Make the explanation no more complex than it needs to be.'

Leonardo da Vinci, a little later, said something broadly similar: 'Simplicity is the ultimate sophistication.'

Albert Einstein had his own version on the simplicity theme: 'Everything should be made as simple as possible, but no simpler.'

 Finally, if you are looking for some contemporary inspiration on how to keep complex things simple, try looking at any of the famous TED talks by Hans Rosling. He is a scientist and mathematician who has made it his mission to present data about social, economic and health issues clearly and concisely. Visit here to see for yourself:

http://www.ted.com/speakers/hans_rosling

Try the Twitter test

Most of us have a kind of love-hate relationship with Twitter. It can be so annoying and boorish. But, at the same time, the sheer discipline of trying to express an idea or an issue in 142 characters is a wonderful one.

Have a go at summarising your strategic initiative as a tweet. To find out if you have passed the Twitter test, you need to ask others if they can understand your initiative in this super-simplified form.

Draw it on the back of a napkin

Dan Roam, a US management consultant (www.danroam.com), has written a number of books on the topic of using *visual language* to express ideas. His first – and in many ways his best – is *The Back of the Napkin*. In this, he explains the importance of being able to explain an idea on the back of a napkin in a restaurant or café.

We love the book and the idea. Not surprising, really, as in many ways this book is designed to work out in exactly that way:

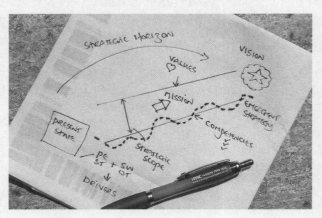

We designed the napkin image to explain how we think strategy fits together – and prefer it to the PowerPoint version in **Step 1**. Try it with your own strategy. All you need is a pen and a napkin!

growing your strategic mindset and skillset

Not just ideas

This might seem to be a book about ideas. It is more than that. Strategy is not just about ideas. It is about people. The people who have those ideas and the people on whom they impact.

If you want to really grow and become excellent at strategy – both mindset and skillset – you may want to find someone who can help you grow and develop in confidence and competence.

Having a development partner offers a number of advantages:

- It gives you someone to bounce ideas off.
- They can ask you challenging questions.
- They can offer you support.
- You can ask for advice.
- They can help you consider issues systematically.

They can also have some potential disadvantages:

- You can become dependent on them.
- They may offer their own opinion too often.
- They may offer weak advice or guide you poorly.
- They may not challenge you enough.

On balance, we think the advantages outweigh the disadvantages. But, choosing a person is a strategic decision, so you need to be systematic about it

What kind of partner?

A development partner can take one of a number of forms or fulfil one of a number of roles. You may need all of them at some point in your strategic development journey, which means finding a number of buddies.

- **Mentor:** someone who focuses on helping you develop your career. The main aim is to help you progress. You may need a mentor to advise you when it is best to move jobs to develop your skills as a strategist. Sometimes, you can get stuck in an organisation, unable to progress. A mentor can help you make a good move.

- **Coach:** someone who is concerned with your performance in your current role. They are more likely to help you think about how best to develop a project or scheme that you are working on. They will focus on what is appropriate and fit for purpose – even if it is not very interesting to you or does not help you move on.

- **Consultant:** someone who offers you technical advice on a tool or technique, for example. An external consultant working in your organisation might be able to give you a strong technical grasp of one of the techniques in the book. If a chance like that comes up, seize it. You will, almost certainly, benefit.

One person might help in all three roles. But it would be an exceptional individual who could do them all well. You are probably better off with different buddies for different roles.

Who ya gonna call?

So, having decided what kind of person you need, you should seek out the right individual to offer you support. Do not just jump for the first available person or, indeed, your favourite social friend.

Consider:

- senior managers in your organisation
- senior managers outside your organisation
- peers you respect from within the team or department
- people on various coaching registers through LinkedIn or the local Chamber of Commerce.

Consider, too, people who are not like you:

- someone of a different gender
- someone of a different cultural background
- someone from a different industry
- someone from a different discipline – for example, from R&D, if you are in marketing.

Some of the most creative and useful set-ups can come from connections with people who are very different to you. The otherness also means you are much less likely to get someone who shares your own prejudices and exceptions. A good person does not just sympathise – they also challenge and offer another perspective.

Organising the session

The session will be more successful if you put in some effort and organise it a bit:

- Find a quiet space – ideally, either out of the office or in a space where you will not be disturbed.
- Maybe think about different seating – something more comfortable than the usual office chairs – or possibly, even, walking and talking.
- Have a flipchart or whiteboard – or even a sketchpad – available. Lots of strategic conversations end up in drawings.
- Coffee, tea, camomile infusion, water, orange juice or even Diet Coke will help fuel the event. What it is is not really important, but make sure you have something to drink.
- Set aside an appropriate time, maybe early in the day while your brain is fresh and you are not worrying about the emails you have to answer.

There is no question that face-to-face interaction is best. But, if that is not possible, find a person who can work with you online. (This might make it easier to find someone who is very different from you.)

Preparation

Before you meet your development partner, you should both do some preparation to gain the most from the session.

- **You:** consider the specific issue you want to address. What is it? Why is that issue important now? Do you need to clarify what the real issue is? Do you have a view or a solution that you want to check out? Or do you want to work through the challenge using a specific tool? What is the outcome you want – a decision, some choices to ponder? How should you set this up to make sure the conversation is productive?

- **Buddy:** are you the right person? What has this person asked you to address? Can you add value to that conversation? In what way might there be any challenges to you being involved? Consider the specific issue they want to address – what is it? Why is that issue important to them? Do they have a view or a solution that they want to check out? Or do they want to work through the challenge using a specific tool? What is the outcome they want – a decision, some choices to ponder? What is the right set-up for this discussion?

Follow up

When the session is finished, it should end up with one of you writing up notes on:

- what learning took place during the session
- what actions were agreed and who will do them
- when the next session is
- what action will happen in between.

Development programme

As part of your personal strategic development programme, probably you want to arrange to meet your partner several times over a few months – perhaps five or six sessions in all.

The following structure might help to shape the sessions, if you want to look at a specific issue:

Session	Purpose
1. Define the development need.	Analysis of the issues to work on – what is it you are trying to address? Is that appropriate?
2. Establish who are key stakeholders.	Decide who is important in this process – and what is their relationship to you?
3. Devise options for consideration.	Build up one or more strategic options with advantages and disadvantages.
4. Decide on an option and roll out.	Make a judgement on the best-fit option and then focus on how to roll it out.
5. Track emerging impact.	Collect appropriate data to judge if the strategy is on track.
6. Evaluate the impact of your intervention.	Consider how effective you have been in terms of improving business and your position.

Learn everywhere

You might also work on more general application of your strategic knowledge.

- Stop playing *Candy Crush* or watching re-runs of *Game of Thrones* on the train in the morning. Buy a copy of the *Financial Times* or another newspaper, and look for strategic decisions being made or unmade.

- Subscribe to *Harvard Business Review* (*HBR*) or the slightly funkier *Fast Company* and read an article about strategy once a week. *HBR* always carries a case study and asks various experts to analyse it.

- Create a strategy version of a book club. So, collect a number of peers and distribute a case study – again available from *HBR* online – and discuss it over a coffee or during lunchtime.

Other kinds of buddying

There are other kinds of buddying aside from the classic one-to-one approach. You might like to consider the following.

Virtual coaches

Put together a group of imaginary advisors who are able to offer you advice, even though they are not actually there. This might include:

- historical figures – Julius Caesar or Elizabeth I
- famous business people: Bill Gates or Richard Branson
- famous politicians: Franklin D. Roosevelt or Mrs Thatcher
- figures from literature: Sherlock Holmes or Lizzie Bennet from *Pride and Prejudice.*

The advantages of virtual helpers are:

- you can call on the very best minds
- you can call on them whenever you want
- you can ask them any question you want
- they are free!

All you need to do is to decide what you want to talk about and then, in your imagination, put yourself in a room with the most appropriate character available to advise you:

- Lizzie Bennet for how to speak your mind without offending
- Richard Branson for how to execute strategy with style
- Julius Caesar for how to outmanoeuvre the competition.

(By the way, if this technique seems too flaky, it has been used by a number of very serious people, including Hillary Clinton. She used a team of virtual advisors to advise her when she was feeling embattled in the White House.)

Action learning sets

An action learning set (ALS) is a group of 5–7 people – usually peers or those at a similar level of responsibility and experience. They meet regularly to find practical ways of addressing the real-life challenges they face and to support their own learning and development. Uniquely, set members are encouraged to find their own solutions to challenges and issues through a structured process of insightful questioning by their peers, combined with a balance of support and challenge. But, it is not just a talking shop – it is a practical approach to problem solving.

ALS is a powerful development tool that provides:

- a safe environment where you can explore your own real-life and work challenges, problems, issues and opportunities
- a means of addressing specific issues, which also challenges how you think about those issues
- opportunities to learn from others' experience and to see things from different perspectives.

Twitter

Most strategy gurus are on Twitter – from Rosabeth Moss Kanter to Jim Collins and even the legendary Tom Peters. You can follow them and receive titbits of knowledge and wisdom by reading their views. A number of them often comment on breaking stories, so you can get live confirmation or contradiction of your views. You might even be able to have an exchange with them.

 By the way, you can follow us:

Bernard Ross@bernardrossmc

and

Clare Segal@claresegalmc

and our company

@MgmtCentre

However you decide to fill the development partner role, before you leave the book, take a moment to reflect on your journey. Revisit this questionnaire and compare your answers with the first time, to see how you have developed or improved your overall strategic ability. And, if you need a refresher on anything, remember you can always revisit the relevant solution chapter(s) and re-read it – or them.

1. **How confident are you to express your ideas in a strategic discussion?**

0 1 2 3 4 5 6 7 8 9 10

Want to improve your score? Look back at **Step 1 + Challenge 2, Challenge 10**

2. **How easily can you use strategic tools to analyse your current situation?**

0 1 2 3 4 5 6 7 8 9 10

Want to improve your score? Look back at **Step 2, Step 3 + Skill 9, Skill 10**

3. **How easy do you find it to imagine alternative big picture futures?**

0 1 2 3 4 5 6 7 8 9 10

Want to improve your score? Look back at **Step 5, Step 8 + Skill 7 + Challenge 4**

4. How sure are you that you can identify who is key in your strategy?

Want to improve your score? Look back at **Step 6 + Skill 2, Skill 6, Skill 8**

5. How clear are you on how to turn strategy into step-by-step action?

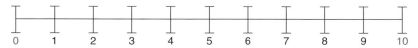

Want to improve your score? Look back at **Step 7, Step 9 + Skill 9, Skill 10**

6. How happy are you selling challenging ideas to others?

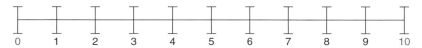

Want to improve your score? Look back at **Step 4, Step 10 + Skill 1, Skill 2, Skill 3 + Challenge 2, Challenge 6**

7. How able are you to identify where to focus your energy and intellect?

Want to improve your score? Look back at **Step 7 + Skill 3 + Challenge 6, Challenge 9**

8. How able are you to think the unthinkable and respond to it?

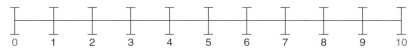

Want to improve your score? Look back at **Step 2, Step 3 + Skill 9, Skill 10**

9. **How ready are you to identify and deal with sources of resistance?**

Want to improve your score? Look back at **Step 2, Step 3 + Skill 9, Skill 10**

10. **How confident are you to name and explain the work of strategic gurus?**

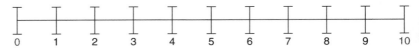

Want to improve your score? Look back at **Step 1 + Skill 9, Skill 10 + Challenge 5**

11. **How strong and positive is your personal brand?**

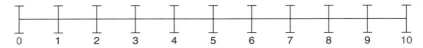

Want to improve your score? Look back at **Step 9 + Skill 4 + Challenge 7, Challenge 8**

12. **How sure are you that you can manage risk – personal and organisational?**

Want to improve your score? Look back at **Step 3 + Skill 3 + Challenge 7, Challenge 8**

13. **Can you use strategic tools confidently to analyse your current situation?**

Want to improve your score? Look back at **Step 2, Step 3, Step 7 + Skill 9, Skill 10 + Challenge 5**

14. **How sure are you that you can manage organisational risk?**

Want to improve your score? Look back at **Step 2, Step 3 + Skill 7 + Challenge 9, Challenge 10**

15. **How good are you at expressing complex ideas simply and clearly?**

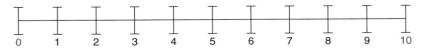

Want to improve your score? Look back at **Steps 1, 9 + Skills 1, 5 + Challenge 7.**

What did you think of this book?

We're really keen to hear from you about this book, so that we can make our publishing even better.

Please log on to the following website and leave us your feedback.

It will only take a few minutes and your thoughts are invaluable to us.

www.pearsoned.co.uk/bookfeedback

A Team, The (film) 137–8
abilities see competencies
action learning sets (ALS) 211
action plans 107, 112–13
activities, urgent and important
    198–201
Adams, Douglas 141
Adams, Scott 5, 117
advice and support 196
    action learning sets (ALS) 211
    development partners 205–9
    Twitter 210
    virtual coaches 210
after action reviews 163–4, 184
agility 194
    see also pivoting
AI see appreciative inquiry (AI)
Aldi 187
Alexander the Great 18
Alice in Wonderland (Carol) 19
ALS see action learning sets (ALS)
Amazon 16, 24–6, 74–5, 111
ambition 170
analogue metrics 109
analysis 30–9, 42
    fishbone 164–7
    Ishikawa 164–7
    personal SWOT 169
    PEST 11, 31, 32–6
    present state 11
    SWOT 11, 31, 32, 36–9
    trends 55–6
    WBAWIN (what business are we
      in) 30–1
Ansoff, Igor 73, 75, 77, 156–7
Ansoff matrix 73–5, 77–81, 157
Apollo 13 (film) 142

Apple 6–7, 70, 76, 152, 180
appreciative inquiry (AI) 164
Argyris, Chris 185
audiences, identifying 122–5,
    129–30

Back of the Napkin, The (Roam) 204
balanced scorecards (BSCs) 96–8,
    157
    see also strategy maps
beliefs see values
benchmarking 11
Bield 47–50
black-hat thinking 88, 89, 91
black swan events 140–4
Black Swan, The (Taleb) 140
blame 163
Blockbuster 189
blue-hat thinking 90, 91
blue ocean strategies 151–5, 157
Body Shop 154, 155
boredom 77
brainstorming 42, 83–6, 89
brand 65, 67, 76
branding, personal 168–73, 194
breast cancer charities 152
British Red Cross 61–2
BSCs see balanced scorecards
    (BSCs)
buddying 205–9, 210–11
budget categories 67
burning platforms 126–8
Burns, Robert 140–1
business models, pivoting 178–81
business process reengineering
    157
buyers 68, 69, 70

calculated risks 191
capital 76–7
card company case study 78–80
Carol, Lewis 19
cash 76–7
Catholic Church 182
cause and effect 99, 164–7
challengers 145, 146, 149
champions 145, 146, 147
Champy, James 157
Chanel, Coco 54
change
    black swan events 140–4
    five5Cs of 145–50
    Good to Great model 158
    Kotter's stages of 158
    transformational 140–4, 158
Change Masters, The (Kanter) 158
changeaphobics 145, 146–7,
    149–50
checklists
    drivers 45
    Ishikawa analysis 166–7
    PEST analysis 35–6
    6Cs checklist of choice xvi, 76–7
chewing gum 179
Children Creche Company 69–71
choices 73–81, 174–7
    10:10:10 formula 176–7
    Ansoff matrix 73–5, 77–81, 157
    card company case study 78–80
    exercises 78, 80–1
    explaining difficult 126–8
    fast and slow thinking 175–6,
        177
    impact and importance matrix
        174–5
    6Cs checklist of choice xvi, 76–7
Cirque du Soleil 152, 157, 185
Clausewitz, Carl von 5
Cluff, Angela 152
coaches 196, 206
    virtual 210
    see also development partners
Coca-Cola 64, 189
Collins, Jim 158, 211
commitment xix, 77, 107

communicating strategy 13
    audiences 122–5, 129–30
    email headlines 124
    explaining difficult choices
        126–8
    impact and importance matrix
        175
    informally 202–4
    KISS 203
    messages 131–3, 134–6
    PR strategies 129–33
    and responses to change 145–50
    think, feel and do (TFD) 134–6
    see also pitches
companions see stakeholders;
    teams
competencies xviii, 10, 14, 24–5
    and decision making 75, 76
    personal 170
competition xviii–xix, 64–71, 76
    Children Creche Company case
        study 69–71
    developing competitive
        advantage 65–6
    exercises 64, 66
    Five Forces Model 68–9, 156
    levels of 66–7
competitive advantage 65–6
competitors 68, 69, 71
compliance risks 191
connectors 130
considerers 145, 146, 148
consultants 182–4, 206
context xvii, 76
converts 145, 146, 148–9
Covey, Stephen 198, 200
crafting strategy 8–9
creative thinking 89, 91
    see also innovation
credibility 172–3
critical success factors 97
critical thinking 88, 89, 91
Cunningham, Barry 55
customer care case study 110
customers xvii
    Ansoff matrix 73–5, 77–81, 157
    cycle times 108, 109, 110, 187–8

Darwin, Charles 181
data, volume of 202
de Bono, Edward 86, 87
de Vlamingh, Willem 140
Decca Recording Company 54
decision making 73–81, 174–7
    10:10:10 formula 176–7
    Ansoff matrix 73–5, 77–81, 157
    card company case study 78–80
    exercises 78, 80–1
    fast and slow thinking 175–6, 177
    impact and importance matrix
        174–5
    6Cs checklist of choice xvi, 76–7
Deepwater Horizon oil spill 189
delaying 195
Delphic model 41
development partners 196, 205–9
development plan, personal
        205–11
    action learning sets (ALS) 211
    development partners 205–9
    reading 209–10
    using Twitter 211
    virtual coaches 210
discovery-driven planning 159
discrimination 168, 172
diversification strategies 75, 78, 79
double loop learning 185–8
dreams 59–60
drivers 42–51
    checklist 45
    engaging staff 51
    exercise 51
    external 44, 45, 48–9
    identifying 44–6
    internal 44, 45, 49–50
    residential care company case
        study 47–50

eBay 22
Ebola epidemic 191
economic factors 32, 35–6
8Ps checklist 166–7
Einstein, Albert 188, 203
elevator pitches 118, 119, 135
Elop, Stephen 128

email headlines 124
emergent strategy 8, 157
End of Competitive Advantage, The
    (McGrath) 159
engagement 19, 51, 134, 136
Enron 23–4
Excel software 113
excitement 77
executive summaries 125
exercises
    black swan events 143–4
    choices 78, 80–1
    competition 64
    competitive advantage 66
    drivers 49–50
    Gantt charts 113
    metrics 111
    scenario planning 58–60
    strategy maps 101–4
    SWOT analysis 38–9
    thinking outside the box 93–4
    VMVC framework 27
    WBAWIN (what business are we
        in) 30–1
experts
    consulting 41
    getting future wrong 54–5
    see also consultants
external context risks 191
external drivers 44, 45, 48–9
external stakeholders 123

facilitating 90, 91
facts, focusing on 87, 91
fast and slow thinking 175–6, 177
Fast Company 209
feelings, focusing on 88, 91
fishbone analysis 164–7
Five Forces Model 68–9, 156
5Cs of change 145–50
Ford, Henry 21
Ford Motor Company 19, 21
Four Actions Framework 153–5
4Ts methodology 192
Francis, Pope 182
Fukushima Daiichi Nuclear Power
    Plant 191

Funky Business (Ridderstråle and Nordström) 158
futurology *see* scenario planning

Galileo 46
Gantt charts 112–13
Gantt, Henry 112
Gates, Bill 54
Geldof, Bob 20
generic strategies 156
Gladwell, Malcolm 130–1
golden egg fable 200
Good to Great model 158
Google 22
Google Glass 189
Gordon, Eric 172
green-hat thinking 89, 91, 195
group activities
    brainstorming 42, 83–6, 89
    Delphic model 41
    driver identification 44–6
    Ishikawa analysis 164–7
    MoSCow method 42
    Six Thinking Hats technique 86–94
Groupon 178
groupthink 41
gurus 156–9, 211

Haig, Douglas 54
Hammer, Michael 157
Harvard Business Review (HBR) 13, 209
heuristics 175–6
Hillshire Brands 12, 13
Hitchhiker's Guide to the Galaxy, The (Adams) 141
honesty 172–3
horizon, strategic 11–12
How the Mighty Fall (Collins) 158
how/why logic 98–9, 101
Humphrey, Albert 31
hype, avoiding 19

IBM 178
imaginative thinking 89, 91
    see also innovation

impact and importance matrix 174–5
impact assessment 192, 195
important and urgent activities 198–201
incentives 107, 112, 196
indicators 107–11
informal communications 202–4
information, volume of 202
innovation 83–94
    brainstorming 42, 83–6, 89
    exercise 93–4
    Motorola case study 92–3
    Six Thinking Hats technique 86–94
insurance case study 34
internal drivers 44, 45, 49–50
internal stakeholders 123
International Federation of Red Cross 61, 97, 163–4
intuition 7–8
Ishikawa analysis 164–7
Ishikawa, Kaoru 165
iTunes 180

John Lewis 15
Johnson, Kelly 203
Jones, Edward 172
Juvenal 140

Kahneman, Daniel 175, 177
Kanter, Rosabeth Moss 111, 126, 158–9, 211
Kaplan, Robert 97–8, 99, 157
key issues
    Delphic model 41
    MoSCow method 42
    see also drivers
key success factors (KSFs) 174–5
killer questions 120–1
Kim, W. Chan 151, 157
KISS 203
Kotter, John 158
KSFs *see* key success factors (KSFs)

lag indicators 108–11
language school case study 65
lead indicators 108–11

Lean Startup methodology 179
Lehman Brothers 189
Lenovo 178
Leonardo da Vinci 131–3, 203
Lepra 178
likelihood assessment 192–3, 195
logical approach 7–8
London 7/7 bombings 60–2

McGrath, Rita 159
McKinsey Consultants 182
Macmillan Cancer Support 178
mandates, team 138–9
market development strategies 74, 78, 79
market penetration strategies 74, 77–9
market position 68
markets, Ansoff matrix 73–5, 77–81, 157
matrices
    Ansoff 73–5, 77–81, 157
    impact and importance 174–5
    priorities 198–201
Mauborgne, Renée 151, 157
mavens 130–1
Mead, Margaret 137
measures 107–11
Médecins Sans Frontières (MSF) 13, 14
membership, team 138–9
mentors 196, 206
    see also development partners
metrics 107–11, 112
Microsoft 20, 128
Mintzberg, Henry 8, 157
mission 10, 12, 21–2, 25
    team 138–9
mobile phones xx
momentum 107–13
    customer care case study 110
    exercises 111, 113
    metrics 107–11, 112
    motivation 107, 111–12, 196
    movement 107, 112–13
Morrisons 187
MoSCow method 42

motivation 107, 111–12, 196
Motorola 92–3
movement 107, 112–13
MSF see Médecins Sans Frontières (MSF)

napkin-based strategy 202–4
narratives 58
new entrants 68, 69–70
nightmares 59–60
Nobel Prize 175–6
Nokia 127–8
Nordström, Kjell 158
Norton, David 97–8, 99, 157

objectives, in strategy maps 99, 100–1, 103–4
Occam's razor 203
Odeo 180
offering development strategies 75, 78, 79
offerings 67
    Ansoff matrix 73–5, 77–81, 157
    substitute 68, 69, 70
online surveys 51
opportunities 36–8
    personal 169
organisational risk see risk management

partners 196, 205–9
PepsiCo 21
performance management systems 191
performance risks 191
personal branding 168–73, 194
personal development 205–11
    action learning sets (ALS) 211
    development partners 205–9
    reading 209–10
    using Twitter 211
    virtual coaches 210
personal risk management 194–6
personal SWOT analysis 169
PEST analysis 11, 31, 32–6
Peters, Tom 77, 211
Piper Alpha oilrig disaster 126–7

pitches 117–21
  elevator 118, 119, 135
  group 117–18
  killer questions 120–1
  one-to-one 119–20
pivoting 112, 178–81
planning, discovery-driven 159
planning, scenario see scenario
  planning
planning strategy 8–9
political factors 32, 35–6
Porter, Michael 31, 67–8, 156, 159
positive psychology 164
positive thinking 88–9, 91
post mortems 163–7
  after action reviews 163–4, 184
  appreciative inquiry (AI) 164
  Ishikawa analysis 164–7
PR strategies 129–33
present state analysis 11
priorities 197–201
priorities matrix 198–201
procrastination 195
products 67
  Ansoff matrix 73–5, 77–81, 157
  substitute 68, 69, 70
prospect theory 177
public relations strategies 129–33

questionnaire, self-assessment
  xxii–xxv, 212–15
questions
  answering up front 125
  challenging personal 171–2
  killer 120–1

rapport 119
Red Cross 61–2, 97, 163–4
red-hat thinking 88, 91
red ocean strategies 151, 153, 157
reflection 188
research 119
residential care company case
  study 47–50
reviews 163–7
  after action reviews 163–4, 184
  appreciative inquiry (AI) 164

of consultancy effectiveness
  184
  Ishikawa analysis 164–7
rewards 112, 196
Ridderstråle, Jonas 158
Ries, Eric 179
risk averse/risk seeking mindsets
  177
risk management 189–93
  4Ts methodology 192
  impact and likelihood 192–3, 195
  personal 194–6
  risk aware mindset 190
  types of risk 191
Roam, Dan 204
Rosling, Hans 203

salespeople 131
Sara Lee 12, 13
Save the Children 22
scenario planning 54–62
  exercise 58–60
  London 7/7 bombings case
    study 60–2
  reasons for 56–7
  stages 57–8
  versus trends analysis 55–6
Schön, Donald 185
scope see strategic scope
scorecards
  balanced 96–8, 157
  impact and importance matrix
    175
self-assessment questionnaire
  xxii–xxv, 212–15
senior management
  consulting 41
  as development partners 206
  and new ideas 54
  as PR targets 129–30
  see also stakeholders
services 67
  Ansoff matrix 73–5, 77–81, 157
  substitute 68, 69, 70
7 Habits of Highly Effective People,
  The (Covey) 198
sexism 172

Shell 55
Shepway District Council 97
Shipping News, The (film) 118
simplicity
    in communicating strategy 202–4
    elevator pitches 118, 119, 135
    KISS 203
    in vision statements 20
Simpsons, The 191
Sinclair C5 189
single loop learning 186–8
Six Thinking Hats technique 86–94
6Cs checklist of choice xvi, 76–7
skills see competencies; personal
    development
social factors 32–3, 36
South West Airlines 99–101
stakeholders xix–xx, 7, 77
    consulting 42
    external 123
    identifying 122–5, 129–30
    internal 123
    keeping informed 112
    key success factors for 174–5
    see also senior management
Star Trek 7–8, 9
strategic drivers 42–4
    checklist 45
    engaging staff 51
    exercise 51
    external 44, 45, 48–9
    identifying 44–6
    internal 44, 45, 49–50
    residential care company case
        study 47–50
strategic foresight 55
strategic hindsight 55
strategic horizon 11–12
strategic scope 15–16
strategy
    crafting 8–9
    definitions 4–5
    emergent 8, 157
    levels 5–6
    need for 18
    planning 8–9
    preferences 7–9

thinking strategically 4–9
    see also VMVC framework
strategy gurus 156–9, 211
strategy maps 96, 98–104
    exercises 101–4
    how/why logic 98–9, 101
    South West Airlines case study
        99–101
    see also balanced scorecards
        (BSCs)
strategy teams 137–9
strengths 36, 37
    personal 169
substitute products and services
    68, 69, 70
supermarkets 187
suppliers 68, 69, 70
support and advice 196
    action learning sets (ALS) 211
    development partners 205–9
    on Twitter 210
    virtual coaches 210
Survey Monkey software 51
surveys 51
SWOT analysis 11, 31, 32, 36–9
    personal 169
System 1 and System 2 thinking
    175–6, 177

Taleb, Nassim 140, 142–3
talent 137–9
talent tweets 138
targets 109, 112
Tate Gallery 34
teams xx, 7, 137–9
technological factors 33, 36
10:10:10 formula 176–7
terminate risks 192
Tesco 187
think, feel and do (TFD) 134–6
thinking
    fast and slow 175–6, 177
    reflection 188
    strategically 4–9
    see also thinking outside the box
Thinking, Fast and Slow
    (Kahneman) 175–6

thinking outside the box 83–94
  brainstorming 42, 83–6, 89
  exercise 93–4
  Motorola case study 92–3
  Six Thinking Hats technique
    86–94
  threats 37–8
    personal 169
time management 198
Tipping Point, The (Gladwell) 130–1
tolerate risks 192
training, risk preparation 192
transfer risks 192
transformational change 140–4,
  158
trends analysis 55–6
Tversky, Amos 177
Twitter 138, 180, 204, 211

unexpected events 140–4
urgent and important activities
  198–201
US Army 163–4
USP (unique selling proposition)
  170
utility theory 177

values 10, 13, 22–4, 25–6
  personal 170

virtual coaches 210
vision 10, 11, 19–21, 25
visual language 204
VMVC framework 10–14, 18–27,
  103
  Amazon case study 25–6
  competencies xviii, 10, 14, 24–5
  exercise 27
  mission 10, 12, 21–2, 25
  values 10, 13, 22–4, 25–6
  vision 10, 11, 19–21, 25

Watson, Tom 54
WBAWIN (what business are we in)
  30–1
weaknesses 36, 37
  personal 169, 172–3
'What if' questions 121
When Giants Learn to Dance
  (Kanter) 159
white-hat thinking 87, 91
WIFM (what's in it for me) 122–5
William of Ockham 203
Wrigley's chewing gum 179

yellow-hat thinking 88–9, 91

Zara 187–8
Zen 188